Gluten-Free One-Mix
Main Courses

Gluten-, Dairy-, and Soy-free
Recipes for Everyday Dinners

By Diane M. Kuehn, PhD

With recipes by
Laura Cinquemani-Rojahn

Nutrition analysis by
Joan Nicholson, MA, CAS, RD, CDN, FAND, CHES

ISBN-13: 978-1735527529

Photographs by Diane Kuehn

Recipe testing by Mark Kuehn

Deposited in the Library of Congress

Printed in the United States of America

Bad Cat Baking Company LLC
Central Square, NY
badcatbakingcompany.com

Dedication

To my parents, Alice and Joe, and Mother-in-law, Anne –
your strength, love, and support have always been my
foundation in life. Thank you!

Acknowledgements

Many thanks to all those who helped with and inspired the recipes for this cookbook. Mark and Sean: I love you both. You continue to inspire my recipes. I also appreciate your willingness to taste-test and critique new recipes. Special thanks to Sean for designing the Bad Cat Baking logo! My parents and Mother-in-Law for providing new dietary limitations to challenge my recipe-writing skills. My sister, Laura, who was kind enough to share two of her wonderful entrée recipes for this book (Laura is definitely the chef of the family – I am a mere baker). My brother, Joe – always a willing taste-tester. All of the Rojahns and Kuehns for their constant support and encouragement. Ginny and Pete for their willingness to try my early attempts on a regular basis, and for their encouragement to create the Bad Cat Baking Company.

And finally, to Joan Nicholson for her constant encouragement and friendship, and for doing the nutrition analysis for this book. Her comments and insight have always inspired me to do my best to boost the nutrition in my recipes. Joan, I'm looking forward to a future of four-hour lunches with you! Thank you!

Disclaimer

The contents of this cookbook (such as text, recipes, nutritional analyses, graphics, and images) are for informational purposes only and do not provide any medical advice. The contents of this book are not intended as a substitute for professional medical advice, diagnosis, or treatment. Always seek the advice of your physician or other qualified health provider with any questions you have regarding a medical condition, before making any major changes to your diet, and before using any of the recipes or information in this book. Never disregard professional medical advice or delay in seeking it because of information you have read in this book. It is solely the reader's choice to use any of the recipes and information contained in this book. The author, consulting Registered Dietitian, and publisher are not responsible for any outcomes, results, or other consequences of the reader's use of the contents of this book. The author, consulting Registered Dietitian, and publisher do not recommend or endorse any specific medical tests, physicians, health care providers, or products mentioned in this book.

Always make sure that all the ingredients you use for these recipes are free of gluten, dairy, and soy, as well as any other items to which you are allergic or intolerant. It is important to note that some of the recipes in this book, though made with nutritious flours, can be high in calories, sugar, and saturated fat. Before making any recipe, consult with a professional healthcare provider to determine if it and its ingredients are suited to your health concerns and those of your family.

About the Nutrition Analysis

The nutrition analysis information listed at the end of each recipe was estimated by Joan Nicholson, a Registered Dietician and retired Professor at the State University of New York at Morrisville, using The Food Processor® software version 11.1.0 by ESHA Research, Inc. (2015). This software bases its nutritional estimates on the USDA food composition tables. Each recipe was analyzed for estimated caloric, carbohydrate, dietary fiber, sugar, protein, fat, dietary fiber, and sodium content. The nutrition analyses for recipes also include the content of other nutrients and minerals, such as iron and calcium; small amounts of other nutrients which are not listed may also exist in the recipes. Estimates are rounded to the nearest whole number.

Some other points are important to note concerning the nutrition data included in this cookbook. First, this nutrient content information should be used as a general guide only, since results can vary from the estimates provided depending on the brands of ingredients used, type of processing of the flour (e.g., sprouted vs. regular flours), cooking techniques used (e.g., deep frying at too low a temperature will cause the flour to absorb more oil), and accuracy of ingredient measurements. Second, if a choice of ingredients is given in a recipe (e.g., "shortening or lard"), the first ingredient listed is the one included in the nutrition analysis. Third, the estimates are based on the use of almond milk as the dairy-free "milk of choice," palm oil shortening as the shortening, and olive oil or canola oil as the oil; using a different type of milk of choice, shortening, or oil will change the nutrient content. Fourth, the word "sugars" denotes all sugars (e.g., fructose, glucose, sucrose, maltose) and includes the natural sugars found in fresh and dried fruit, as well as those in sweeteners such as honey, maple syrup, and cane sugar. Finally, any changes made to these recipes (including following any of the "Allergy/Intolerance Substitutions" or "Reduced Sugar" suggestions) will change the nutritional content of the baked goods from what is listed.

Table of Contents

Abbreviations and Conversions

Common Abbreviations:

GF   Gluten-free
DF   Dairy-free
SF   Soy-free
c.   Cup
T.   Tablespoon
t.   Teaspoon
oz.   Ounce
g   Gram
mg   Milligram
mcg   Microgram
l   Liter
ml   Milliliter
cm   Centimeter
mm   Millimeter
"   Inch(es)
F   Fahrenheit
C   Celsius
IU   International Unit

Some useful conversions:

1 Tablespoon = 3 teaspoons
¼ cup = 4 Tablespoons
1 quart = 0.95 liters
1 ounce = 28.3 grams
Oven temperatures: 375° F = 191° C; 350° F = 177° C; 325° F = 163° C

Foreword

This book started with the gift of a pasta machine from my husband. I had always wanted to learn how to make homemade pasta, so I began by experimenting on pastas made with the gluten free flour mix as well as different ingredients such as kale, garlic, and egg substitutes. After several attempts, I developed the basic linguine recipe include in this book. From there, I added kale to make a bright green pasta that is as healthy to eat as it is beautiful to look at. I moved on to creating dumpling recipes such as dairy-free ravioli, gnocchi, and pierogi. This cookbook was born!

I decided to add other main courses that are favorites in my home. My recipes for Not-your-childhood Fish Cakes, Empanadas, and Crispy Fried Chicken came together quickly. With some creative recipes contributed by my sister, Laura Cinquemani-Rojahn, I was able to add flavorful entrées such as the Ginger and Garlic Noodle and Chicken Piccata. And of course, there are the sides of fresh, hot Italian bread, herbed olive oil dipping sauce, hush puppies, and moist turkey meatballs! For those who do not tolerate tomato-based pasta sauces but can eat sweet red peppers, I include my roasted red pepper pasta sauce.

These are recipes I make frequently at home for dinner. I hope you enjoy them as much as my family does!

13

Back to the Basics

Gluten Free Flour Mix Recipe

The gluten free flour mix recipe in this first chapter is reprinted here from my first book, *Gluten-free One-Mix Baking: The Easy Way to Bake without Gluten, Dairy, or Soy*[1]. Though making your own flour mix saves money and is the best taste-wise, you can use an off-the-shelf gluten free mix for these recipes. If you decide to use a store-bought mix, make sure it includes whole grain gluten-free flours and a starch. Xanthan gum is also a useful ingredient that improves the texture of gluten free baked goods; you can bake without it but your baked goods may be slightly crumbly. If xanthan gum is not included in a store-bought mix, simply add 1 teaspoon of xanthan gum to every cup of flour used in the recipe you are making.

☑ **Allergy/Intolerance Substitutions:**
<u>All:</u> Xanthan gum is produced from sugars derived from wheat, dairy, soy, or corn. Check with the manufacturer to determine if the brand you choose is free of your allergens of concern. Use guar gum as a substitute if needed, or leave out completely if you cannot find a safe brand.
<u>Rice:</u> Replace the brown or white rice flour with an equal measure of amaranth flour, and replace the sweet rice flour (which is more similar to a starch than a flour) with an equal measure of arrowroot or tapioca starch.
<u>Nightshade family:</u> Replace the potato starch with either arrowroot starch or tapioca starch.

---

[1] Recipe source: Kuehn, D. (2020). *Gluten-Free One-Mix Baking: The Easy Way to Bake Without Gluten, Dairy, or Soy*. Second edition. Bad Cat Baking Company LLC: Central Square, NY.

Histamine: Do not use buckwheat flour as a substitute for the flours in this recipe. If potato starch is not tolerated, replace it with either arrowroot starch or tapioca starch (if tolerated). Leave out the xanthan and guar gums if not tolerated (no replacement; your final baked goods may be slightly crumbly). Be sure to check with your medical practitioner concerning the use of all ingredients in this flour mix.

Salicylates: Do not use corn flour, corn meal, almond meal, or other nut meals as a substitute for the flours in this recipe. If potato starch is not tolerated, replace it with either arrowroot starch or tapioca starch (if tolerated). If sorghum flour is not tolerated, replace it with either amaranth or quinoa flour as tolerated. Leave out the xanthan and guar gums if not tolerated (no replacement; your final baked goods may be slightly crumbly). Be sure to check with your medical practitioner concerning the use of all ingredients in this flour mix.

Ingredients:

1 c. sorghum flour (120 g)

1 c. brown or white rice flour (120 g)

1 c. sweet (glutinous) rice flour or other finely-ground rice flour (should be the texture of corn starch; 120 g)

1 c. millet flour (136 g)

2⅔ c. potato, arrowroot, or tapioca starch (328 g)

4 t. baking soda (sift to remove clumps if necessary; 20 g)

2 T. xanthan gum or guar gum (20 g)

Directions:

Step 1. Measure the ingredients by scooping with the appropriate measuring cup or spoon, and leveling off with the flat edge of a knife. Place the ingredients in a gallon-sized zipper bag. Seal the bag tightly and shake till the ingredients are well combined.

Step 2. Make sure to shake the bag to re-combine the ingredients before each use. Because of the heaviness of gluten-free flours, sifting the flour mix prior to use generally does not make a noticeable difference in the finished product.

Nutritional content: Makes 7 servings (1 cup or 153 g per serving). Each serving contains: Calories (519 kcal); Total Fat (2 g); Saturated Fat (0 g); Cholesterol (0 mg); Sodium (800 mg); Total Carbohydrate (121 g); Dietary Fiber (6 g); Sugars (0.5 g); Protein (6 g). Nutrient(s) of note: Iron (2 mg), Magnesium (21 mg), Phosphorus (59 mg), Potassium (127 mg).

Egg Replacer Recipes

Although store-bought egg replacers or substitutes are available in most large supermarkets and online, they are easy and inexpensive to make at home. Five different egg replacers are included in this chapter, reprinted here from my first cookbook[2]. Use the new recipe for Egg Wash Substitute to give a nice brown shine to breads, buns, and other baked goods; the Rising Egg Replacer in cakes, breads, and other baked goods that need to rise; the Non-rising Egg Replacer in cookies and pie dough; and the Flax Meal and Chia Seed Egg Replacers in granola and heavy breads. Because the Rising and Non-rising Egg Replacer recipes have been specially created for this book, they tend to work better than store-bought egg replacers for these recipes.

The amount of egg replacer to use is identified throughout this book for each recipe. In general, ¼ cup (59 ml) of egg substitute (provided by each of the egg replacer recipes in this chapter) equals about one large egg. Recipes containing egg replacers may require a longer baking time than needed for the original recipes. These egg replacers should not be used as a substitute for the egg whites in meringue, or as an egg substitute in quiche or omelets.

---

[2] Chapter source: Kuehn, D. (2020). *Gluten-Free One-Mix Baking: The Easy Way to Bake Without Gluten, Dairy, or Soy*. Second edition. Bad Cat Baking Company LLC: Central Square, NY.

1. Egg Wash Substitute
Use in place of a traditional egg wash to give a dark golden-brown shine to sweet or savory baked goods.

☑ Allergy/Intolerance Substitutions:
<u>Tree nuts (coconut):</u> Replace the coconut milk with a milk of choice that has a high fat content.
<u>Histamine:</u> Avoid if you do not tolerate collagen or gelatin.
<u>Porcine/Bovine:</u> Use vegan collagen powder in place of the powdered gelatin.

Directions:
Prepare this Egg Wash no more than ten minutes before baking. Microwave 3 T. (45 ml) of full-fat coconut milk with 1 T. honey (22 g) in a small microwave-safe bowl for **30 seconds**; whisk to dissolve the honey. Sprinkle 1 t. (2.5 g) unflavored, powdered gelatin or vegan collagen on the coconut milk/honey mixture; whisk to dissolve. Brush *liberally* on baked goods; immediately place the baked goods in the oven to bake.

2. Chia Seed Egg Replacer
Use for hearty breads and granola.

☑ Allergy/Intolerance Substitutions:
<u>Histamine:</u> Avoid if you do not tolerate chia seeds.
<u>Salicylate:</u> Avoid this recipe.

Directions:
Whisk 2 t. (6 g) of chia seeds with 3 T. plus 1 t. (50 ml) hot tap water for one minute. Let the mixture thicken for **10 minutes**, stirring occasionally, before adding to your recipe. Though chia seed often works better as an egg replacer than flax meal, the small seeds can make baked goods look spotted and may add an unwanted crunch.

3. Flax Meal Egg Replacer
Use for hearty breads and granola.

☑ Allergy/Intolerance Substitutions:
Histamine: Avoid this recipe.
Salicylate: Avoid this recipe.

Directions:
Living Without's: Gluten-free & More magazine provides an easy flax meal egg replacer recipe. Whisk 1 T. (6.5 g) flax meal with 3 T. (45 ml) hot tap water. Let the mixture thicken for **10 minutes**, stirring occasionally.[3]

4. Rising Egg Replacer
Use for baked goods that need to rise (i.e., cakes, breads, scones, and pizza dough).

☑ Allergy/Intolerance Substitutions:
Bovine/Porcine: Use agar powder instead of gelatin.
Histamine: If tolerated: use quinoa flour instead of bean flour; use agar powder instead of gelatin or leave out; and replace the apple cider vinegar with distilled white vinegar or leave out.
Salicylate: If tolerated, use garbanzo bean flour and unflavored, powdered gelatin (fava/broad bean flour and agar powder are high in salicylates, as are many flavored gelatins). Leave out the apple cider vinegar.

---

[3]"Substitution Solutions," *Living Without's Gluten-free & More Magazine,* June/July 2015, p. 109.

Ingredients:
⅓ c. bean flour (garbanzo or fava) or quinoa flour (40 g)
¼ c. arrowroot starch (30 g)
⅓ c. tapioca starch (44 g)
1 T. baking powder (15 g)
1 t. baking soda (5 g)
1½ t. unflavored gelatin powder or agar powder (4.5 g)
1 t. apple cider vinegar (5 ml)

Directions:
Step 1. Mix together the dry ingredients (i.e., all ingredients except for the vinegar) in a 2-cup (½-liter) storage container. Store the sealed container at room temperature till use. Shake to recombine the ingredients prior to use.

Step 2. For the equivalent of one egg, whisk together in a small bowl the egg replacer powder and water as follows:

> *For recipes labeled specifically as "cakes":*
> 1 T. (6 g) egg replacer powder with 3 T. (45 ml) water.

> *For other recipes requiring the "Rising Egg Replacer":*
> 2 T. (12 g) egg replacer powder with 2 T. (30 ml) water.

Step 3. Let the mixture rest at room temperature for **5 minutes**; whisk again.

Step 4. Whisk in 1 t. (5 ml) apple cider vinegar per "egg," and immediately add the egg replacer to the batter. (Note: this egg replacer loses its "lift" if allowed to rest after adding the vinegar; bake as directed in the recipe as soon as the batter is mixed.)

5. Non-rising Egg Replacer
Use for cookies and doughs that do not need to rise.

☑ Allergy/Intolerance Substitutions:
Bovine/Porcine: Use agar powder instead of gelatin.
Histamine: If tolerated, use quinoa flour instead of bean flour, and use agar powder instead of gelatin or leave out completely.
Salicylate: If tolerated, use garbanzo bean flour and unflavored, powdered gelatin (fava/broad bean flour and agar powder are high in salicylates, as are many flavored gelatins).

Ingredients:
⅓ c. bean flour (garbanzo or fava) or quinoa flour (40 g)
¼ c. arrowroot starch (30 g)
⅓ c. tapioca starch (44 g)
1½ t. unflavored gelatin powder or agar powder (4.5 g)

Directions:
Step 1. Mix together the ingredients in a 2-cup (½-liter) storage container. Store the sealed container at room temperature till use. Shake to recombine the ingredients prior to use.

Step 2. For the equivalent of one egg, whisk in a small bowl 2 T. (12 g) of the egg replacer powder with 2 T. (30 ml) of water. Let the mixture rest at room temperature for **5 minutes**.

Step 3. Whisk prior to adding to your recipe. (Note: do not add apple cider vinegar as specified in the Rising Egg Replacer recipe.)

A Side of Bread

Hush Puppies

Served warm, hush puppies (fried dough balls) are meant to be a side dish. These have become a main course in my home. Crisp on the outside, soft inside, and slightly sweet with bits of bacon (optional), corn, and onion, these are irresistible! Makes about 1 dozen.

Hands-on preparation time: 45 minutes
Total preparation time: 60 minutes

☑ Allergy/Intolerance Substitutions:
Egg: In step 4, replace the egg with one Non-Rising Egg Replacer (see page 25).
Nightshade family: Leave out the jalapenos in step 2.
Corn: Avoid this recipe.
Porcine: In step 2, leave out the bacon or replace with a vegan variety.

☑ Reduced sugar:
In step 4, replace the Tablespoon (22 g) of honey with 15 drops of alcohol-free liquid stevia.

Dough ingredients:
2 quarts oil with a high smoke point (1.9 liters)
2 slices raw bacon (optional; 45 g)
1 raw cob of corn
1 medium onion (approx. 100 g)
1 jalapeno (25 g)
1 c. corn meal (132 g)
¾ c. gluten free flour mix (96 g)
1 t. baking powder (5 g)
1 t. salt (6 g)
½ t. black pepper (1.5 g; optional)
1 large egg
1 T. honey (22 g)
1¼ c. milk of choice (296 ml)
1 T. apple cider vinegar (15 ml)

Directions:
Step 1. Pour the oil into a large sauce pan (the oil should be about one inch (2.5 cm) deep); heat on a **medium** burner. The oil will need to reach a temperature of **350° F/177° C** by step 6.

Step 2. As the oil is heating, fry the bacon till crisp; cool on a paper towel, and then crumble into small pieces. Slice the corn off the cob. Mince the onion. Cut the stem off the jalapeno, slice the pepper in half lengthwise, remove and discard the seeds, and then mince.

Step 3. Mix together the corn meal, gluten free flour mix, baking powder, salt, and black pepper in a large mixing bowl.

Step 4. In a small mixing bowl, whisk together the egg, honey, milk of choice, and vinegar. Add to the dry ingredients and mix well with a rubber spatula to make a smooth, thick batter.

Step 5. Mix the bacon, corn, minced onion, and minced jalapeno into the batter with a rubber spatula. Let the batter rest for **15 minutes.**

Step 6. Once the oil has reached **350° F/177° C**, fry the hush puppies in two separate batches. For the first batch, scoop up about 1 Tablespoon (17 g) of batter with a small cookie scooper; release the scoop into the heated oil. Repeat for four to five other scoops of batter. Each scoop of batter will expand to golf ball size as it fries. Using a slotted metal spoon, gently separate the hush puppies in the hot oil to prevent them from sticking together.

Step 7. Cook the hush puppies in the hot oil for **1½ to 2 minutes** till the bottom of each turns a deep golden brown. Using the slotted spoon, gently flip and cook the other side for **another 1½ to 2 minutes** till deep golden brown. Carefully remove the hush puppies from the hot oil with the slotted spoon and place them on a paper-towel-lined plate to drain.

Step 8. Bring the temperature of the oil back to **350° F/177° C.** Repeat steps 6 and 7 for the remaining batter. Serve warm.

☑ Nutritional Content:

Makes 6 servings (2 hush puppies per serving).
Each serving contains: Calories (260 kcal); Total Fat (10 g); Saturated Fat (2 g); Cholesterol (42 mg); Total Carbohydrate (38 g); Dietary Fiber (3 g); Sugars (5 g); Sodium (574 mg); Protein (5 g). Nutrient(s) of note: Vitamin A (163 IU), Beta-carotene (45 mcg), Calcium (178 mg), Iron (1.4 mg), Magnesium (82 mg), Potassium (170 mg).

Whole-Grain Italian Bread and Burger Buns

If you're looking for a tasty bread that comes out similar in texture to Italian bread, then try this recipe. Though darker in color than regular Italian bread (we're using nutritious flours here), it has a light texture and mild flavor. Makes one standard loaf, eight burger buns, or two baguettes.

Hands-on preparation time: 20 minutes
Total preparation time: 1 hour and 50 minutes

☑ Allergy/Intolerance Substitutions:

Eggs: In step 2, replace the 2 eggs and 2 egg whites with 3 Rising Egg Replacers (page 23) plus 1 Tablespoon (15 ml) of water. Leave out the apple cider vinegar specified in the egg replacer recipe since vinegar is already included in the bread recipe. Leave off the egg wash in step 6.

Bovine/Porcine: In step 1, use powdered, unflavored agar instead of gelatin.

Yeast: Avoid this recipe.

☑ Reduced Sugar:
Do not reduce the amount of honey in this recipe; it is needed to activate the yeast.

Ingredients:
3 c. gluten free flour mix (390 g)
1 c. arrowroot starch or tapioca starch (120 g)
1 T. powdered, unflavored gelatin or agar (7.5 g)
2 t. table salt (12 g)
2¼ t. **Rapid Rise** instant yeast (one packet; 9 g)
2 large eggs
2 egg whites from large eggs (80 g)
1¾ c. warm tap water (414 ml)
5 T. olive oil or other neutral-flavored oil (75 ml)
2 t. apple cider vinegar or distilled white vinegar (10 ml)
2½ T. honey (55 g)
1 egg yolk for egg wash (18 g; optional)

Pre-heat oven: warm (lowest setting)

Directions:
Step 1. In a large mixing bowl, mix together all of the dry ingredients (including the yeast) with a rubber spatula.

Step 2. In a medium-sized mixing bowl, whisk together the two eggs, two egg whites, warm tap water, oil, vinegar, and honey. Pour this liquid mixture into the dry ingredients; mix with the rubber spatula till well combined and smooth (no lumps; **1 to 2 minutes**).

Step 3. Spray a double French loaf pan or large loaf pan (5" x 9", or 13 cm x 23 cm) with cooking oil. To make hamburger buns, place eight 3.5-inch (9 cm) diameter

English muffin rings on a parchment-lined cookie sheet; spray the inside of each ring with cooking spray.

Step 4. <u>If using the double French loaf pan:</u> Spread half of the dough evenly on each side of the pan till it is about 2 inches (5 cm) from either end of the pan. Smooth the top of the both loaves with a rubber spatula. Use a sharp knife to make 5 to 6 diagonal slices (½ inch or 1 cm deep) across the top of each loaf.

<u>If using the large loaf pan:</u> Spread the dough evenly in the pan. Smooth the top of the dough with a rubber spatula. Use a sharp knife to make 4 to 5 diagonal slices (½ inch or 1 cm deep) across the top of the loaf.

<u>If using the English muffin rings on a cookie sheet:</u> Divide the dough equally between the eight rings. Spread the dough out in each ring and smooth the top with a rubber spatula.

Step 5. Spray the top of the dough with cooking spray. Cover the dough with a sheet of plastic wrap. **Turn off the oven.** Put the loaves in the warmed oven, and let them rise till nearly doubled in size (about **35 to 40 minutes)**.

Step 6. Remove the pan from the oven. Pre-heat the oven to **350° F/177° C.** Remove the plastic wrap from the dough. Brush the top of the dough with an egg wash (optional) made from 1 egg yolk whisked with 1 Tablespoon (15 ml) of water. Place the pan or cookie sheet back in the oven; bake till golden brown and a toothpick inserted in the center of the loaf or buns comes out clean (approximately **45 to 50 minutes** for the baguettes or hamburger buns, and **50 to 55 minutes** for the large loaf).

Step 7. Remove the bread from the oven and let cool for **15 minutes**. Slide a knife between the bread and the pan or rings, and then carefully remove the bread from the pan or rings; place the bread on a cooling rack. Cool for **30 minutes** more before slicing. Enjoy with some Garlic and Herb Olive Oil Dip (page 117)!

☑ Nutritional Content:
<u>Standard loaf:</u> Makes 9 servings (1 thick slice per serving). Each serving contains: Calories (311 kcal); Total Fat (10 g); Saturated Fat (2 g); Cholesterol (63 g); Total Carbohydrate (52 g); Dietary Fiber (2 g); Sugars (5 g); Protein (6 g). Nutrient(s) of note: Vitamin A (89 IU), Phosphorus (54 mg), Potassium (66 mg), Sodium (778 mg).

<u>Baguettes:</u> Makes 24 servings (1 slice per serving). Each serving contains: Calories (117 kcal); Total Fat (4 g); Saturated Fat (1 g); Cholesterol (24 mg); Total Carbohydrate (19 g); Dietary Fiber (1 g); Sugars (2 g); Protein (2 g). Nutrient(s) of note: Vitamin A (33 IU), Sodium (292 mg), Phosphorus (20 mg), Potassium (24 mg).

<u>Hamburger buns:</u> Makes 8 servings (1 bun per serving). Each serving contains: Calories (350 kcal); Total Fat (11 g); Saturated Fat (2 g); Cholesterol (71 g); Total Carbohydrate (58 g); Dietary Fiber (2.5 g); Sugars (5 g); Sodium (878 mg); Protein (6 g). Nutrient(s) of note: Vitamin A (100 IU), Phosphorus (63 mg), Potassium (79 mg).

Crispy Bread Sticks

These hearty bread sticks come out crisp and flavorful – just right for any evening meal. Makes about 14 bread sticks.

Hands-on Preparation Time: 25 minutes
Total Preparation Time: 1 hour and 25 minutes

☑ Allergy/Intolerance Substitutions:

Tree nuts (almonds, coconut):
In step 1, replace the almond meal with a homemade seed meal made by food-processing shelled pumpkin seeds or sunflower seeds till finely ground. In step 2, replace the coconut cream with 3 Tablespoons of any thick milk of choice.

Eggs: Prepare the equivalent of one whole egg using the Non-rising Egg Replacer (page 25). In step 3, replace the egg with the egg replacer.

☑ Reduced Sugar:

In step 3, replace the honey with 10 drops of clear, alcohol-free liquid stevia.

Preparation in advance:

Refrigerate one 13.5-oz. (400 ml) can of full-fat coconut milk for at least **2 hours** or as long as overnight before starting this recipe.

Dough ingredients:
1½ c. gluten free flour mix (195 g)
½ c. arrowroot or tapioca starch (60 g)
¼ c. bean flour or quinoa flour (30 g)
¼ c. almond meal (25 g)
½ t. baking powder (2.5 g)
½ t. table salt (3 g)
⅓ c. shortening or lard (50 g)
⅓ c. coconut cream (82 g) from one 13.5-oz. (400 ml) can
　　of coconut milk (full fat)
1 large egg
1 T. honey (22 g)
¼ c. water (59 ml), plus extra for moistening if needed
2 T. finely chopped fresh rosemary or basil (4 g)
1 T. kosher salt (18 g)
1 T. sesame seeds (9 g)
1 t. garlic powder (3 g)

Directions:
Step 1. Mix the dry ingredients together in a large mixing bowl or the bowl of a large food processor.

Step 2. Add the shortening/lard and coconut cream to the dry ingredients; cut in with a pastry cutter or by pulsing in the food processor, until the flour is grainy in texture.

Step 3. In a small mixing bowl, whisk the egg with the honey, ¼ cup (59 ml) of water, and the fresh rosemary or basil. Pour into the flour/shortening mixture; mix with your hands or the food processor till the dough pulls together into a ball that is uniform in texture and easy to knead. If the dough is slightly dry and crumbly, mix in one to two extra teaspoons (5 to 10 ml) of water. Knead the dough by hand for an additional minute till it is smooth.

Step 4. Form the dough into a ball and wrap it in wax paper. Let the wrapped dough rest at room temperature for **15 to 30 minutes.** (Note: if the room temperature is above 70° F/21° C, place in a cool location but not the refrigerator). **Pre-heat the oven to 350° F/177° C.**

Step 5. Place a 12" x 15" (30 cm x 38 cm) piece of plastic wrap on the counter. Place the dough on top of the plastic wrap. Cut a piece of parchment paper to fit a cookie sheet. Lay the parchment paper on top of the dough. Roll out the dough to form a rectangle that is roughly 7" x 10" (18 cm x 25 cm) in size and ½-inch (1 cm) thick. Use the side of your hand to smooth the edges. The dough needs to be as close to a rectangle in shape as possible.

Step 6. Flip the dough over onto the cookie sheet, so that the parchment paper is in direct contact with the cookie sheet and the plastic wrap is facing up. Remove and discard the plastic wrap. Cut the dough into ½-inch-wide (1-cm-wide) strips with a pizza cutter.

Step 7. Gently lift one end of a dough strip, twist it once *away* from you, and place it back down on the parchment paper. Next, lift the other end of the dough strip, but twist it *towards* you this time. Adjust the twists so that they are evenly spaced along the length of the dough strip, and so that the strip is fairly straight. Repeat for the remaining dough strips, spacing the strips about ½-inch (1 cm) apart on the cookie sheet. (Note: you will need to move some of the strips to the ends of the cookie sheet so that you have enough room to space the strips out).

Step 8. Brush the strips of dough with the egg wash, egg wash substitute (see page 22), or melted coconut cream. Sprinkle the dough with the kosher salt, sesame seeds, and garlic powder.

Step 9. Bake for **25 to 30 minutes**, till the bread sticks are crisp and brown. Let cool for **5 minutes**. Use a metal spatula to move the bread sticks from the cookie sheet to a cooling rack. Enjoy warm or at room temperature.

☑ Nutritional Content:
Makes 12 servings (1 bread stick per serving).
Each serving contains: Calories (172 kcal); Total Fat (7 g); Saturated Fat (2.5 g); Cholesterol (15 mg); Total Carbohydrate (25 g); Dietary Fiber (1 g); Sugars (5 g); Sodium (788 mg); Protein (2 g). Nutrient(s) of note: Vitamin A (30 IU), Calcium (54 mg), Potassium (27 mg).

Garlic Kale Crackers

If you like kale, you will love these crackers; if you don't like kale, see if this recipe changes your mind! They are crispy, with a mild sweetness that mellows the slightly bitter flavor of the kale. You will need a food processor to make this recipe. Makes about 60 one-inch-square crackers.

Hands-on preparation time: 15 minutes
Total preparation time: 60 minutes

☑ **Allergy/Intolerance Substitutions:**
Tree nuts (almonds, cashews): In step 1, use shelled sunflower or pumpkin seeds instead of almonds or cashews.

☑ **Reduced Sugar:**
In step 1, replace the honey with 20 drops of clear, alcohol-free liquid stevia.

Dough ingredients:

0.6 ounces kale leaves (no stems; 18 g)
1 medium clove garlic (6 g)
½ c. gluten free flour mix (65 g)
¼ c. raw almonds or cashews, or shelled pumpkin or
sunflower seeds (38 g)
1 T. fresh lemon zest (2 g)
⅛ t. table salt (0.7 g)
2 T. olive oil (30 ml)
2 T. honey (44 g)
½ t. kosher salt (3 g)
½ t. sesame seeds (1 g)

Preheat oven: 325° F/163° C

Step 1. Place all of the ingredients (<u>except</u> for the kosher salt and sesame seeds) in a large food processor; process for **1 minute**. Scrape the sides of the food processor bowl and process for **1 minute** more to form a sticky dough.

Step 2. Place a piece of plastic wrap that is 12" x 15" (30 cm x 38 cm) in size flat on a counter. Cut a piece of parchment paper to fit a cookie sheet.

Step 3. Scrape the kale dough out of the food processor bowl and place it in the center of the plastic wrap. Lay the sheet of parchment paper on top of the dough. Using a rolling pin on top of the parchment, roll out the dough till it is ⅛"-thick (3 mm) and approximately 7" x 9" (18 cm x 23 cm) in size. (Note: be sure to not roll the outer edges of the dough too thin; the edges should be the same thickness as the center of the dough to ensure even baking.)

Step 4. Flip the sheet of dough (with the parchment attached) upside-down onto a cookie sheet; the parchment will now be in direct contact with the cookie sheet and the plastic wrap will be facing up. Using a smooth pastry wheel *on top of* the plastic wrap, deeply score the sheet of dough to form squares that are approximately one-inch-square (2.5-cm-square) in size. Score along the edges of the dough to separate any rough edges from the squares. To keep the score lines straight, roll the pastry wheel along the edge of a ruler. Avoid cutting the plastic wrap with the pastry wheel.

Step 5. Peel back the plastic wrap and sprinkle the top of the dough with the kosher salt and sesame seeds. Place the plastic wrap back on top of the dough; lightly press on the plastic wrap with your hands to embed the salt and seeds in the dough. Remove and discard the plastic wrap.

Step 6. Place the cookie sheet in the oven. Bake **20 to 22 minutes** till the crackers turn a *light* greenish brown in color. (Note: do not over-bake; the crackers bitter tasting if baked till dark in color). Remove the crackers from the oven and cool for **5 minutes**.

Step 7. Use a metal spatula to slide the sheet of crackers off the parchment and onto a cooling rack. Cool for **20 minutes** more. Gently break the crackers apart along the score lines. Store in a sealed container at room temperature for up to one week.

☑ Nutritional Content:

Makes 6 servings (10 crackers per serving).
Each serving contains: Calories (141); Total Fat (8 g); Saturated Fat (1 g); Cholesterol (0 mg); Total Carbohydrate (16 g); Dietary Fiber (1 g); Sugars (6 g); Sodium (304 mg); Protein (2 g). Nutrient(s) of note: Vitamin A (300 IU), Beta-carotene (178 mcg), Calcium (25 mg), Vitamin K (24 mcg), Potassium (32 mg).

Sweet Curry Crackers

These sweet potato crackers have a mild and slightly spicy curry flavor. If you don't tolerate the spices, switch them out for 1 to 2 Tablespoons (3 to 6 g) of dry herbs such as tarragon or thyme. You will need a food processor to make this recipe. Makes about 100 crackers.

Hands-on preparation time: 20 minutes
Total preparation time: 80 minutes

☑ **Allergy/Intolerance Substitutions:**
<u>Tree nuts (almonds):</u> In step 2, replace the raw almonds with ¼ cup (38 g) of either shelled sunflower seeds or pumpkin seeds.
<u>Nightshade family:</u> In step 2, leave out the cayenne pepper.

☑ Reduced Sugar:
In step 3, replace the Tablespoon of honey with 10 drops of clear, alcohol-free liquid stevia. The crackers will not brown as well with this substitution.

Dough ingredients:
1 small sweet potato (130 g)
½ c. gluten free flour mix (65 g)
¼ c. sweet rice flour (30 g)
¾ t. baking powder (4 g)
¼ c. raw almonds (38 g)
½ T. dried ground ginger (4.5 g)
¾ t. ground turmeric (2 g)
½ t. cinnamon (1.5 g)
½ t. cumin (1.5 g)
¼ t. cayenne powder (0.7 g)
⅛ t. table salt (0.7 g)
2 T. olive oil (30 ml)
1 T. honey (22 g)
½ t. sesame seeds (1 g)

Preheat oven: 325° F/163° C

Directions:
Step 1. Peel the sweet potato and cut into large chunks. Place the chunks in a food processor and process for **1 minute** till finely chopped.

Step 2. Add the gluten free flour mix, sweet rice flour, baking powder, almonds, powdered spices, and table salt to the food processor. Process for **1 minute**.

Step 3. Add the olive oil and honey to the food processor bowl. Process for **1 minute** till the dough pulls together into a ball.

Step 4. Place a 12" x 15" (30 cm x 38 cm) sheet of plastic wrap on the counter. Scrape the dough out of the food processor bowl and onto the center of the plastic wrap. Cut a piece of parchment paper to fit a cookie sheet. Place the parchment on top of the dough.

Step 5. Using a rolling pin *on top of* the parchment paper, roll out the dough into a rectangle that is ⅛" (3 mm) thick and approximately 9" x 12" (23 cm x 30 cm) in size. Make sure the middle of the dough is the same thickness as the edges to ensure even baking.

Step 6. Flip the sheet of dough (with parchment attached) upside-down onto a cookie sheet so that the parchment is now in direct contact with the cookie sheet and the plastic wrap is facing up. Use a smooth-edged pastry wheel *on top of the plastic wrap* to deeply score the sheet of dough into 1" x 1" (2.5 cm x 2.5 cm) squares. Score along the edges of the dough to remove any rough edges from the squares. To keep the score lines straight, roll the pastry wheel along the edge of a ruler. Avoid cutting the plastic wrap with the pastry wheel.

Step 7. Peel back the sheet of plastic wrap and sprinkle the sesame seeds on top of the dough. Put the plastic wrap back into place and lightly press on it with your hands to embed the sesame seeds in the dough. Peel off and discard the sheet of plastic wrap.

Step 8. Place the cookie sheet in the oven. Bake **25 to 30 minutes** till the crackers are crisp and brown. Remove from the oven and cool at room temperature for **5 minutes**.

Step 9. Using a metal spatula, slide the sheet of crackers off the parchment paper and onto a cooling rack. Cool for **20 minutes** more.

Step 10. Gently break the sheet of crackers apart into squares along the scored lines. Let cool uncovered overnight for the crispest crackers. Enjoy!

☑ Nutritional Content:

Makes 10 servings (10 crackers per serving).
Each serving contains: Calories (102 kcal); Total Fat (5 g); Saturated Fat (0.5 g); Cholesterol (0 mg); Total Carbohydrate (13 g); Dietary Fiber (1.5 g); Sugars (2.5 g); Sodium (69 mg); Protein (1.5 g). Nutrient(s) of note: Vitamin A (1875 IU), Beta-carotene (1122 mcg), Calcium (98 mg), Magnesium (30 mg), Potassium (62 mg).

Home-style Poultry Stuffing

I decided to reprint this recipe from my first cookbook[4] because stuffing makes a great side dish or (in my house) stand-alone meal. A loaf of Applesauce-Oat Sandwich Bread (from my first book) is used as the base, but the Whole-Grain Italian Bread on page 33 works just as well for this recipe. Makes 12 servings.

Hands-on preparation time: 30 minutes
Total preparation time: 2 to 4.5 hours, depending on baking method

---

[4] Recipe source: Kuehn, D. (2020). *Gluten-Free One-Mix Baking: The Easy Way to Bake Without Gluten, Dairy, or Soy.* Second edition. Bad Cat Baking Company LLC: Central Square, NY.

☑ Allergy/Intolerance Substitutions:
Eggs: Prepare the equivalent of one egg using the Non-rising, Flax Meal, or Chia Seed Egg Replacer recipe (pages 22-25). In step 6, replace the egg with the egg substitute.
Yeast: Use a yeast-free bread.
Porcine: Replace the Italian sausage with a sausage that meets your dietary needs.

☑ Reduced Sugar:
In step 1, use an unsweetened bread. In step 5, use an unsweetened sausage. In step 6, leave out the dried cranberries if needed.

Preparation the day before: Make one loaf of Applesauce-Oat Sandwich Bread, Whole-Grain Italian Bread (page 33), or other bread of choice.

Stuffing ingredients:
One loaf of Applesauce-Oat Sandwich Bread, Whole-Grain
    Italian Bread, or other bread of choice
2 T. olive oil or other neutral-flavored oil (30 ml)
1 medium onion, chopped
3 celery stalks, chopped
1 green apple, peeled and chopped
3 T. of chopped fresh sage (6 g)
1 pound of GF-DF-SF loose Italian sausage (453 g)
1 large egg
½ c. of dried cranberries (80 g)
Salt and pepper
1 to 2 cups GF-DF-SF chicken broth or vegetable broth (237
    to 473 ml)

Preheat oven: 325° F/163° C

Directions:

Step 1. Use a serrated bread knife to remove the crust from the cooled loaf of bread. Cut the loaf into ¾-inch (2 cm) cubes, and place them on an 11" x 13" (28 cm x 33 cm) baking pan.

Step 2. Bake the cubes for **60 to 80 minutes**, turning them every **15 minutes** with a metal spatula, till all sides of the cubes are dry and crisp to the touch. Do not air-dry the cubes as stale gluten-free bread will not re-soften the same as stale wheat bread when the stuffing ingredients are mixed together.

Step 3. Pour the bread cubes into a large mixing bowl; let them cool to room temperature. Follow your traditional stuffing recipe or continue with the recipe below.

Step 4. Pour 2 Tablespoons (30 ml) of olive oil into a large frying pan. Over **medium heat**, sauté together the chopped onion, chopped celery, and chopped green apple, until the onions become translucent and the celery has softened slightly (**5 to 10 minutes**). Add the chopped sage and sauté for **one minute** more. Pour this mixture into the large mixing bowl with the bread cubes.

Step 5. Place the loose sausage in the frying pan. Cook the sausage over **medium heat**, flipping it with a spatula, until it is completely cooked through. As it cooks, cut it into bite-sized pieces using a fork and knife. Transfer the cooked sausage to a bowl that has been lined with paper towel, and let the sausage drain for a few minutes.

Step 6. To the large mixing bowl, add the cooked Italian sausage, raw egg, dried cranberries, and a little salt and pepper (if the broth or the sausage is already salted, you may need to reduce the amount of salt added). Use a large metal or wooden spoon to gently combine all the ingredients (try not to break the bread cubes as you mix).

Step 7. Slowly add ½ cup (118 ml) of the broth, pouring it in a thin stream over the entire mixture. Using the metal or wooden spoon, gently combine the broth with the stuffing mixture. Let the mixture sit for **one minute** to absorb the liquid. Repeat this process, adding another ½ cup (118 ml) of the broth. Check the bread cubes to see if enough broth has been added (the outside of the cubes should be slightly mushy while the inside remains somewhat firm.) If more broth is needed, add ¼ cup (59 ml) at a time, gently mixing the ingredients together after each addition, until the cubes have been adequately moistened. Be careful not to add too much broth as the bread cubes will become soggy.

Step 8. For moist stuffing, bake the stuffing in a slow cooker on low for about **3 hours**, until the stuffing reaches an internal temperature of **165° F/74° C**. For stuffing with a crisp top, bake as follows: **Pre-heat the oven to 350° F/177° C**. Spray a large (84 oz. or 2.5 liter) casserole dish with cooking oil. Pour the stuffing into the casserole dish and cover. Bake for **40 minutes**. Remove the cover of the casserole dish and bake **10 minutes more**, until the stuffing reaches an internal temperature of **165° F/74° C**.

Nutritional content: Makes 12 servings (¾ cup per serving or 208 g). Each serving contains: Calories (340); Total Fat (13 g); Saturated Fat (3 g); Cholesterol (60 mg); Sodium (705 mg); Total Carbohydrate (45 g); Dietary Fiber (3 g); Sugars (13 g); Protein (11 g). Nutrient(s) of note: Vitamin A (162 IU), Calcium (48 mg), Iron (2 mg), Phosphorus (109 mg), Potassium (282 mg).

Pasta and Dumplings

Vegan Linguine

This pasta comes out tasty and smooth, even though it is egg free. Serve with your favorite pasta sauce, or sauté with a little chopped basil, crushed garlic, and olive oil. You will need a food processor as well as a pasta machine with a linguine attachment to make this recipe. Makes 5 servings.

Hands-on preparation time: 60 minutes
Total preparation time: 80 minutes

☑ Allergy/Intolerance Substitutions:
<u>Tree nuts (coconut)</u>: Replace the coconut water in step 2 with plain water (i.e., a total of 1¼ cups (296 ml) of water will be used in step 2).

☑ Reduced Sugar:
There is no added sugar in this recipe.

Dough ingredients:

2 c. plus 1 T. gluten free flour mix (268 g)
1 c. quinoa flour or bean flour (120 g)
1 c. arrowroot starch or tapioca starch (120 g)
1 t. dried basil (1 g)
1 t. garlic powder (3 g)
½ t. table salt (6 g)
¾ c. tap or filtered water (177 ml)
½ c. coconut water (118 ml)
½ c. arrowroot starch or tapioca starch for dusting (60 g)

Directions:

Step 1. Add the gluten free flour mix, quinoa or bean flour, 1 cup (120 g) of arrowroot or tapioca starch, dried basil, garlic powder, and salt to a large mixing bowl or the bowl of a large food processor. Mix till the flours are combined.

Step 2. Add the water and coconut water to the dry ingredients in the mixing bowl or food processor bowl; mix or process till well combined. Scrape the sides of the bowl with a rubber spatula and then mix for **1 minute more** until the dough pulls together into a ball. If the dough remains crumbly after 1 minute, add 1 teaspoon (5 ml) water and mix longer. Wrap the ball of dough tightly in wax paper and let it rest at room temperature for **20 minutes**.

Step 3. Place the additional ½ cup (60 g) of starch in a small bowl. Dust a 13" x 17" (33 cm x 43 cm) baking pan with a little of this starch. Shake the pan to make sure the bottom of the pan is coated with the starch; set the pan aside. If you plan on cooking the pasta as soon as it is cut, fill a large pot with water and place it on a burner set to **medium**; the water will need to come to a boil by step 9.

56

Step 4. Set up your pasta machine. Set the opening of the pasta machine to its thickest setting for a sheet of pasta. Lightly dust your hands with a little starch from the small bowl. Remove approximately ¼ cup (2.5 oz. or 70 g) of the dough from the wax paper; leave the remaining dough wrapped tightly in the wax paper. Knead the small ball of dough in your hands for **30 seconds**.

Step 5. Flatten the ball of dough so that it is roughly ½-inch (1 cm) thick and about 3 inches (8 cm) wide. Pass the dough through the pasta machine, catching it carefully as it comes through. The dough will fall apart at this point; simply layer it together and pass the layered sheet through the pasta machine again. Fold the sheet of pasta and pass it through the pasta machine a third time. If the dough sticks or feels wet as it goes through the pasta machine, *lightly* dust it with starch (note: don't use too much starch as this will make the pasta tough). To make the edges of the pasta sheet smooth, fold both outside edges of the dough in, towards the middle of the sheet, before passing it through the pasta machine. Repeat this folding and thinning process 4 to 6 more times till the pasta is smooth and the dough sheet is roughly a 5- to 6-inch (13 cm to 15 cm) square. Place the sheet of dough in the pan and sprinkle with a light dusting of starch.

Step 6. Repeat steps 4 and 5 for all of the dough, layering the dough sheets on one side of the pan, and sprinkling a small amount of starch on each layer.

Step 7. Reduce the setting of your pasta machine by one increment. Pass one of the dough sheets through the machine to thin it. Reduce the setting again, and pass the sheet through the pasta machine a second time. Reduce the setting one more time, and pass the pasta through the machine a third time. At this point, the sheet of dough will be moderately thin. Place it in the pan next to the thicker sheets of dough, and sprinkle it with a little starch. Repeat this step for the remaining pasta sheets.

Step 8. Add the linguine cutter to the pasta machine. Pass each sheet of dough through the cutter, catching the pasta as it leaves the machine. Place it in a loose pile in a large baking pan. Repeat this step for the remaining sheets of dough.

Step 9. At this point, you can either cook the pasta immediately or dry it for future use. To dry the pasta, leave it uncovered at room temperature for 24 hours and then place it in a zipper bag or sealed container in the freezer. To cook the pasta, gently place the desired amount of pasta in the boiling water (one large handful is usually enough for one serving). Bring the water back to a boil and cook the pasta till it is *al dente* (slightly firm inside) – about **3 to 5 minutes** for fresh pasta, and **5 to 7 minutes** for dried. Drain the pasta in a colander, rinse, and serve with your favorite sauce.

☑ Nutritional Content:
Makes 5 servings (excludes pasta sauce).
Each serving contains: Calories (406 kcal); Total Fat (2 g); Saturated Fat (0 g); Cholesterol (0 g); Total Carbohydrate (91 g); Dietary Fiber (5 g); Sugars (1 g); Sodium (755 mg); Protein (6 g). Nutrient(s) of note: Calcium (23 mg), Iron (2.6 mg), Phosphorus (24 mg), Potassium (103 mg).

Ginger and Garlic Noodle

This recipe is a creation of my sister's, Laura Cinquemani-Rojahn. It's deceptively simple to make but loaded with a rich, sweet and slightly spicy flavor. If you tolerate soy, try the original recipe by substituting ⅔ cup (158 ml) of gluten free soy sauce (tamari) for the fish sauce, coconut milk, and water. This recipe can be made with either zucchini or steak. Makes enough for 4 people.

Hands-on preparation time: 30 minutes
Total preparation time: 3 hours (includes the time needed to chill the marinade and to marinate the steak or zucchini)

☑ Allergy/Intolerance Substitutions:
Tree nuts (coconut): In step 1, replace the coconut milk with an equivalent amount of another milk of choice. Replace the coconut sugar with light brown sugar.

<u>Nightshade family:</u> Leave out the red pepper flakes in step 1, and red bell pepper in step 5.

<u>Fish:</u> Leave out the fish sauce in step 1, and replace with ½ teaspoon (3 g) fine sea salt, or, if coconut is tolerated, 1 Tablespoon coconut aminos (adjust the salt to taste if using the coconut aminos).

<u>Sesame:</u> In step 1, replace the sesame oil with olive oil. In step 7, leave out the sesame seeds.

☑ Reduced Sugar:
In step 1, replace the coconut sugar with 30 drops of alcohol-free liquid stevia.

Ingredients:
¼ c. organic coconut sugar (36 g)
¼ c. coconut milk (59 ml)
¼ c. water (59 ml)
2 T. GF Thai fish sauce (30 ml)
2 t. sesame oil (10 ml)
½ t. red pepper flakes (1 g)
1 T. grated fresh ginger or ginger purée from a jar (11 g)
6 to 8 garlic cloves, crushed in a garlic press (36 to 40 g)
One 20 oz. (567 g) sirloin steak <u>or</u> one medium-sized
    zucchini (approximately 280 g)
Half of one batch of the Vegan Linguine (page 55) <u>or</u> one
    12-ounce (340 g) package of GF pasta
1 red bell pepper (220 to 230 g)
1 yellow onion (180 to 190 g)
2 T. olive oil (30 ml)
1 T. sesame seeds (9 g)

Directions:
Step 1. In a small sauce pan, mix together the coconut sugar, coconut milk, water, fish sauce, sesame oil, red pepper flakes, grated ginger, and crushed garlic. Bring to a simmer on the stovetop over **medium** heat. Remove the pot from the burner when the sauce begins to bubble; stir to dissolve the sugar. Pour the marinade into a container, cover, and place in the refrigerator to cool.

Step 2. If preparing the zucchini version of this recipe, slice off the ends of the zucchini, and then cut the zucchini into strips that are about 3 inches long, ½-inch (1 cm) thick, and ½-inch (1-cm) wide. If preparing the steak version of this recipe, cut the meat into ¼-inch-thick (6-mm-thick) slices, cutting *across the grain*.

Step 3. Place the slices of steak or zucchini in a zipper bag. Once the marinade has cooled, add approximately one-third of it to the sliced steak or zucchini, and seal the zipper bag; knead the bag to coat the slices with the marinade. Marinate for at least **2 hours or overnight**.

Step 4. About **35 minutes** before the meal is to be served, bring a large saucepan of water to a boil over **high heat**. Cook the pasta according to either the pasta recipe or pasta package instructions. Once the noodles are *al dente* (nearly cooked through but slightly firm in the center), drain and rinse them.

Step 5. As the pasta is cooking, thinly slice the red bell pepper and onion. Sauté the peppers and onions in 2 Tablespoons (30 ml) of olive oil in a large frying pan over **medium heat** till they soften and begin to caramelize (about **10 minutes**). Remove the peppers and onions from the pan.

Step 6. Place the sliced and marinated steak or zucchini in the frying pan. <u>For the steak</u>, cook for **2 minutes** uncovered over **medium heat** till it is just cooked through. <u>For the zucchini</u>, cook covered over **medium heat** for **5 minutes** till tender when poked with a fork.

Step 7. Add the noodles, peppers and onions, and remaining marinade to the frying pan with the steak or zucchini; leave the pan uncovered. Stir until all of the ingredients are heated through (about **1 minute**). Sprinkle with the sesame seeds and serve.

☑ Nutritional Content:

<u>Steak version:</u> Makes 4 servings (includes 85 g of GF pasta per serving). Each serving contains: Calories (795 kcal); Total Fat (28 g); Saturated Fat (8 g); Cholesterol (123 mg); Total Carbohydrate (88 g); Dietary Fiber (6 g); Sugars (14 g); Sodium (1102 mg); Protein (52 g). Nutrient(s) of note: Vitamin A (1905 IU), Beta-carotene (968 mcg), Vitamin B3 (9 mg), Vitamin C (79 mg), Calcium (60 mg), Iron (5.5 mg), Magnesium (58 mg), Phosphorus (370 mg), Potassium (837 mg).

<u>Zucchini version:</u> Makes 4 servings (includes 85 g of GF pasta per serving).
Each serving contains: Calories (530 kcal); Total Fat (16 g); Saturated Fat (4 g); Cholesterol (0 mg); Total Carbohydrate (90 g); Dietary Fiber (6 g); Sugars (15 g); Sodium (627 mg); Protein (11 g). Nutrient(s) of note: Vitamin A (2006 IU), Beta-carotene (1053 mcg), Vitamin C (92 mg), Calcium (57 mg), Iron (2 mg), Magnesium (33 mg), Phosphorus (71 mg), Potassium (482 mg).

Pesto Linguine

Kale, fresh basil, and garlic add flavor and nutrition to this lovely green pasta that even kale haters will like. The kale can be replaced with spinach if preferred. You will need a food processor and a pasta maker for this recipe. I recommend using a food scale for measuring the ingredients to ensure that the proportions of kale to flour are accurate. I use the Roasted Red Pepper Sauce on page 119 with this recipe. Makes enough for 4 light eaters.

Hands-on preparation time: 45 minutes
Total preparation time: 1 hour and 10 minutes.

☑ **Allergy/Intolerance Substitutions:**
Eggs: In step 4, replace the two egg yolks with **half** of one Non-rising Egg Replacer (i.e., when preparing the egg replacer, mix 1 Tablespoon (7 g) of the egg replacer powder with 1 Tablespoon (15 ml) of water; page 25).

☑ Reduced Sugar:
There is no added sugar in this recipe.

Dough ingredients:
1 oz. kale leaves with stems removed (about 3 to 5
    moderately-sized leaves; 28 g)
0.2 oz fresh basil leaves (about 4 to 6 large leaves; 5 g)
1 medium-sized clove of garlic, crushed (about 5 g)
1 c. gluten free flour mix (130 g)
½ c. quinoa flour or bean flour (60 g)
¼ t. table salt (1.5 g)
2 yolks from large eggs
¼ c. water (59 ml)
2 T. tapioca, arrowroot, or potato starch for dusting (15 g)

Directions:
Step 1. Strip the green kale leaves off of their stems;
discard the stems. The leaves should weigh 1 ounce or 28
grams. Wash and blot dry the kale and basil leaves.

Step 2. Add the kale, basil leaves, and crushed garlic clove
to the bowl of a large food processor. Process until finely
chopped (about **30 seconds**). Scrape the sides of the food
processor bowl with a rubber spatula. Continue processing
the mixture until a finely ground paste is made (about **1
minute** more).

Step 3. Add the flours and salt to the food processor. Pulse
till the flours are mixed with the kale/basil paste.

Step 4. Add the egg yolks and water to the food processor;
mix for **30 seconds**. Turn off the food processor and scrape
the sides of the bowl. Process about **1 minute** more until
the dough pulls together into a ball. If the dough remains

crumbly after one minute, add 1 teaspoon (5 ml) water and process **30 seconds** more. Leave the dough covered inside the food processor for **15 minutes**.

Step 5. Dust an 11" x 15" (28 cm x 38 cm) baking pan with 1 Tablespoon (8 g) of the potato, arrowroot, or tapioca, starch; shake the pan to coat the bottom with the starch. Set the pan aside. If you plan on serving the pasta right away, put a large pot containing 4 quarts (3.8 liters) of water on the stove over **medium-high** heat; it will need to come to a boil by step 11.

Step 6. Set up your pasta machine. Set the opening of the pasta maker to its thickest setting. Lightly dust your hands with a little starch. Remove approximately ¼ cup of dough (about 2.5 oz. or 70 g) from the food processor. Briefly knead to pull the dough together into a small ball.

Step 7. Flatten the ball of dough so that it is roughly ½-inch (1 cm) thick and about 3 inches (8 cm) wide. Pass the dough through the pasta machine. The dough will fall apart easily at this point as it comes out of the pasta machine; simply layer it together and pass the layered sheet through the pasta machine again. Fold the sheet of pasta and pass it through the pasta machine 4 to 6 more times till the pasta is smooth. If the dough sticks or feels wet as it goes through the pasta machine, *lightly* dust it with starch (note: don't use too much starch as this will make the pasta tough). To make the edges of the pasta sheet smooth, fold both outside edges of the dough in, towards the middle of the sheet, before passing it through the pasta machine. Gently place the thinned sheet of dough in the starch-dusted pan on one side, and sprinkle with a little starch.

Step 8. Repeat steps 6 and 7 for the remaining dough, layering the dough sheets on one side of the pan, and sprinkling a small amount of starch on each layer.

Step 9. Reduce the setting of the pasta machine by one increment. Pass one of the dough sheets through the machine. Reduce the setting again, and pass the sheet through the machine a second time. Reduce the setting one more time, and pass the pasta through the machine a third time. At this point, the sheet of dough will be moderately thin and 8 to 12 inches (20 to 30 cm) long. Place it in the pan next to the thicker sheets of dough, and sprinkle it with a little starch. Repeat this step for the remaining sheets of pasta.

Step 10. Attach the linguine cutter to the pasta machine. Pass one sheet of dough through the cutter, catching the linguine as it passes through the machine. Place the linguine in a loose pile in a large baking pan. Repeat this step for the remaining sheets of dough.

Step 11. At this point, the linguine can be either dried for future use, or boiled and served immediately. <u>To dry the pasta</u>, leave it uncovered in the pan at room temperature for **24 hours**. Once dry, place it in a zipper bag or sealed container in the freezer. <u>To cook the pasta</u>, gently lay the desired amount in the pot of boiling water; stir to separate. Bring the water back to a boil, stir again, and cook the pasta till it is *al dente* (slightly firm inside) – about **3 to 5 minutes** for fresh pasta, and **5 to 7 minutes** for dried. Drain the pasta in a colander, rinse, and serve with sauce.

☑ Nutritional Content:

Makes 4 servings (about 74 g per serving; excludes pasta sauce). Each serving contains: Calories (215 kcal); Total Fat (4 g); Saturated Fat (1 g); Cholesterol (92 mg); Sodium (427 mg); Total Carbohydrate (40 g); Dietary Fiber (3 g); Sugars (0.5 g); Protein (5 g). Nutrient(s) of note: Vitamin A (888 IU), Beta-Carotene (462 mcg), Calcium (34 mg), Iron (2 mg), Potassium (79 mg).

Sweet Potato Gnocchi

This quick recipe makes very tasty gnocchi (small cup-shaped dumplings) that can either be boiled and served with sauce, or boiled and then sautéed with caramelized onion, garlic, olive oil, and a pinch of kosher salt (my favorite way of eating them). You will need a food processor for this recipe. Gnocchi can be frozen to serve at a later date. Makes enough for three hungry people; when combined with sauteed veggies, it can serve up to five.

Hands-on preparation time: 30 minutes
Total preparation time: 60 minutes

☑ Allergy/Intolerance Substitutions:
This recipe does not contain any of the eight FDA-identified major allergens or corn.

☑ Reduced Sugar:
There is no added sugar in this recipe.

Dough ingredients:

2 to 3 medium-sized sweet potatoes (about 480 g)
¾ c. gluten free flour mix (96 g)
½ c. sweet rice flour (60 g)
½ t. table salt (3 g)
1 T. arrowroot, tapioca, or potato starch (8 g)

Directions:

Step 1. Place the sweet potatoes on a microwave safe plate. Pierce the skin of each potato several times with the tines of a fork. Microwave for **4 minutes**. Flip the sweet potatoes over and microwave **1 to 2 minutes** more, till the potatoes are completely soft when squeezed. Carefully slice the hot potatoes in half and cool till safe to handle (about **10 minutes**).

Step 2. Scoop out the flesh of the sweet potatoes (discard the peels). Measure 1 cup of sweet potato (about 9 ounces or 250 g); reserve any remaining sweet potato for a different recipe. Place the cup of sweet potato in the bowl of a large food processor. Let cool for **20 minutes** more.

Step 3. Pour 4 quarts (3.8 liters) of water into a large sauce pan on the stove over **medium-high** heat. You will need to bring this water to a gentle boil by step 8.

Step 4. Add the gluten free flour mix, sweet rice flour, and table salt to the sweet potato in the food processor. Mix together till a smooth, thick dough forms (there should not be any chunks of sweet potato visible in the dough). Remove the dough from the bowl, and briefly knead it till it is smooth and pliable. If the dough is too sticky (i.e., it sticks to your hands), sprinkle with an extra Tablespoon (8 g) of sweet rice flour and knead till smooth.

Step 5. Sprinkle the bottom of a 9" x 13" (23 cm x 33 cm) baking pan with 1 Tablespoon (8 g) of arrowroot, tapioca, or potato starch. Shake the pan from side to side to coat the inside of the pan with the starch.

Step 6. Cut the dough into quarters. Place one quarter on a clean (un-floured) countertop or cutting board. Roll out the dough with the palms of your hands to form a smooth log that is approximately a half-inch (1 cm) in diameter (note: if the dough cracks, simply pinch it back together). Cut the dough log into 1-inch-long (2.5-cm-long) pieces. Place the pieces in the starch-dusted baking pan. Repeat this step for the three remaining quarters of dough.

Step 7. To make indentations in the gnocchi, hold a fork by its handle in one hand, and roll each gnocchi down the tines of the fork with the other hand. As you roll each piece, gently push the gnocchi into the tines of the fork with your index finger, leaving tine marks on 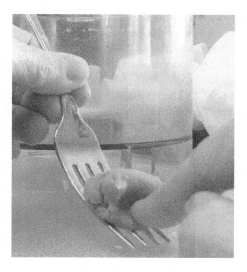 one side and a small cup-shaped indentation from your fingertip on the other side. Repeat for all the gnocchi, placing them back into the baking pan as you work.

Step 8. Once the water in the large saucepan has come to a gentle boil, increase the heat of the burner to **high**. Carefully place the gnocchi in the boiling water and stir to separate (note: depending on the size of your pot, you may need to cook the gnocchi in two batches). Bring the water back to a boil; boil for **3 minutes**, occasionally stirring, till the gnocchi float to the surface of the water and puff up slightly. Remove the gnocchi from the water with a slotted spoon and place them in a colander to drain.

Step 9. Serve immediately with your favorite sauce, or sauté for **1 minute** in olive oil with caramelized chopped onions, garlic, and a pinch of kosher salt. Enjoy!

☑ Nutritional Content:

Makes 3 servings (excludes pasta sauce).
Each serving contains: Calories (326 kcal); Total Fat (1 g); Saturated Fat (0 g); Cholesterol (0 mg); Total Carbohydrate (75 g); Dietary Fiber (6 g); Sugars (7 g); Sodium (642 mg); Protein (5 g). Nutrient(s) of note: Vitamin A (22,699 IU), Beta-carotene (13,614 mcg), Calcium (49 mg), Iron (1.5 mg), Magnesium (44 mg), Phosphorus (88 mg), Potassium (566 mg).

Vegan "Cheese" Ravioli

This amazing recipe is a time consuming one, but for those deprived of cheese, very worthwhile since the cashew-based filling tastes similar to ricotta cheese. You will need a food processor and pasta machine to make this recipe. Directions are given for free-form ravioli, but this recipe works with a ravioli mold as well. The Red Pepper Pasta Sauce (page 119) is also shown in the photo below. Makes 18 large free-form ravioli, enough for 3 to 4 servings.

Hands-on preparation time: 2 hours
Total preparation time: 4 hours

☑ Allergy/Intolerance Substitutions:
Tree nuts (coconut, cashews): In step 2, replace the coconut cream with ¼ cup of a thick milk of choice. In step 6, replace the coconut water with plain water (you will use a total of 1½ cups of plain water in this recipe). If you are

intolerant of cashews, use an alternate ravioli filling in steps 1 through 4. Fillings to consider include mashed sweet potato, or cooked Italian sausage that has been ground into a paste in a food processor.

☑ Reduced Sugar:
There is no added sugar in this recipe.

Preparation in advance:
Place 1 cup (150 g) of raw cashews in a bowl of water to soak at least **2 hours** before beginning this recipe. Place one 13.5-oz (400 ml) can of full-fat coconut milk in the refrigerator at least **2 hours** before beginning this recipe.

Filling ingredients:
1 c. raw whole cashews (150 g)
⅓ c. coconut cream (82 g) from one 13.5-oz. (400 ml) can of full-fat coconut milk
½ T. arrowroot starch or tapioca starch (4 g)
½ t. kosher salt (3 g)
½ t. apple cider vinegar (2.5 ml)
2 T. chopped, fresh parsley (4 g)
1 T. chopped, fresh basil (2 g)
1 t. fresh lemon zest (0.5 g)

Dough ingredients:
2 c. plus 1 T. gluten free flour mix (260 g plus 8 g)
1 c. quinoa flour or bean flour (120 g)
1 c. arrowroot starch or tapioca starch (120 g)
1 t. table salt (3 g)
¾ c. water (177 ml)
½ c. coconut water (118 ml)
½ c. arrowroot starch or tapioca starch for dusting (60 g)

Directions:

Step 1. To make the filling, drain and blot dry the cashews. Place them in a food processer and process for **1 minute** till they reach a fine grain-like consistency.

Step 2. Remove ⅓ cup (82 g) of thick coconut cream from the can of coconut milk; add it to the food processor and process for **1 minute** (reserve the coconut water in the can for step 6). Turn off the food processor and scrape the sides of the bowl with a rubber spatula.

Step 3. Add the ½ Tablespoon (4 g) of arrowroot or tapioca starch, kosher salt, and apple cider vinegar to the food processor. Process for **2 minutes** more (scraping the sides of the bowl halfway through) to make a smooth paste.

Step 4. Move the filling to a medium-sized container. Gently fold in the chopped parsley, chopped basil, and lemon zest. Cover the container and refrigerate for **30 minutes**.

Step 5. Clean and dry the food processor bowl, then prepare the dough. Add 2 cups (260 g) of gluten free flour mix, the quinoa flour or bean flour, 1 cup (120 g) of arrowroot or tapioca starch, and the table salt to the bowl of the food processor. Pulse till the flours are combined.

Step 6. Add ¾ cup of water and ½ cup of coconut water to the food processor bowl with the dry ingredients. Process till well combined. Scrape the sides of the bowl with a rubber spatula and then mix for **1 minute** more till the dough pulls together into a ball. If the dough is very sticky, add the extra Tablespoon (8 g) of gluten free flour and process **1 minute** more to mix it into the dough. Remove the dough from the food processor and press it together into a ball. Wrap the ball of dough tightly in wax paper and let it rest at room temperature for **20 minutes**.

Step 7. Place the additional ½ cup (60 g) of starch for dusting in a small bowl. Dust the bottom of a 13" x 17" (33 cm x 43 cm) baking pan with 1 Tablespoon (8 g) of the starch. Set the pan aside. Fill a small bowl with ½ cup (118 ml) of water; place this bowl and a pastry brush on the counter near where you will be making the ravioli. Set your pasta maker to the thickest setting for pasta. If you plan on boiling the ravioli as soon as they are made, fill a large sauce pot with water and place it on a burner set to **medium** (this water will need to come to a boil by step 15).

Step 8. Remove approximately ¼ cup (2.4 oz. or 67 g) of the dough from the wax paper (keep the remaining dough *wrapped tightly* in the wax paper). Knead the small ball of dough in your hands for **30 seconds**. Flatten the ball of dough so that it is ½-inch (1-cm) thick and about 3 inches (8 cm) square. Lightly dust both sides of the dough with some starch. (Note: if you are using a ravioli template, you may need to adjust the amount of dough used in this step so that the resulting sheet of dough fits the length of your template.) Weighing the dough during this step is recommended to obtain consistently-sized dough sheets.

Step 9. Set the opening of the pasta machine to its thickest setting. Pass the dough through the pasta machine, catching it as it comes through. It will fall apart at this stage, but will pull together with more passes through the pasta machine in subsequent steps.

Step 10. Fold the dough in half and pass this doubled sheet through the pasta machine. Repeat this step 6 to 8 times, turning the dough each time you pass it through the pasta machine, till the pasta is smooth in texture. To get smoother edges, fold both sides of the dough in towards the middle of the dough and then pass it through the pasta maker. If the pasta begins to catch on the sides of the pasta machine or feels damp, sprinkle it *lightly* with a little more starch (note: don't use too much starch – it can make the dough dry and crumbly).

Step 11. Once the sheet of dough looks smooth, reduce the setting of your pasta machine by one increment. Pass the sheet of pasta through the machine to thin it. Reduce the machine setting by one more increment and pass the pasta through a second time. Reduce the machine setting by one more increment and pass the pasta through a third time. Try to pass the dough through so that the sheet of pasta stretches nearly to the full width of the pasta machine by the end of this step; it should also be roughly about 10 inches (25 cm) in length.

Step 12. Place the sheet of dough on a counter that has been lightly dusted with starch. Using a small cookie scooper, scoop out 1 Tablespoon (14 g) of the ravioli filling and place it about 1.5 inches (4 cm) from one end of the dough sheet (see photo on next page). Place another Tablespoon (14 g) of filling on the dough sheet about 1.5 inches (4 cm) away from the first ball of filling; repeat for a third Tablespoon (14 g) of filling (note: the three balls of filling should be lined up in a row down the center of the sheet of dough). Gently flatten each ball of filling to about ½ inch (1 cm) high with your fingertips.

Step 13. Follow steps 8 through 11 to make a second sheet of dough; set it aside on the counter. Dip the pastry brush in the small bowl of water; brush a *small amount* of water on the first sheet of dough around each scoop of filling (the dough should be slightly damp, *not* wet). Carefully place the second sheet of dough over the scoops of filling, lining up the edges of the dough sheets and gently pressing out any pockets of air around the filling as you lay the dough on top. Firmly but gently press the two sheets of dough together around each ball of filling (be careful not to crack the pasta as this will cause the filling to leak out as the ravioli boil).

Step 14. Using a wavy-edged pastry wheel, cut the rough edges off of the dough, leaving a half-inch (1 cm) border of dough around the filling of each ravioli. Cut between the three ravioli with the pastry wheel to separate them (note: be careful not to cut too close to the filling). Gently pinch together the edges of each ravioli to seal tightly. Place the ravioli in the starch-dusted pan. Repeat steps 8 through 14 for the remaining dough.

Step 15. Increase the heat under the pot of water to **medium-high**. Use a large slotted spoon to gently lay half of the ravioli in the boiling water. Bring the water back to a boil, stirring the ravioli frequently, and cook for **5 to 6 minutes** until the ravioli darken slightly in color. Use a slotted spoon to remove the ravioli from the water and place them in a serving bowl or on a plate. Repeat this step for the remaining uncooked ravioli. Serve with your favorite sauce.

☑ Nutritional Content:

Makes 3 servings (6 large ravioli per serving, sauce not included). Each serving contains: Calories (1167 kcal); Total Fat (78 g); Saturated Fat (23 g); Cholesterol (0 mg); Sodium (1259 mg); Total Carbohydrate (91 g); Dietary Fiber (6 g); Sugars (53 g); Protein (28 g). Nutrient(s) of note: Vitamin A (148 IU), Beta-carotene (88 mcg), Calcium (54 mg), Iron (5 mg), Potassium (109 mg).

Potato Onion Pierogi

Pierogi take time to make and master, but they are so worth the effort! These dumplings are filled with mashed potato and onion. I like to sauté them with olive oil and onion to crisp them up after they are boiled, but they are excellent without this extra step as well. Makes about 17 perogies (enough for 3 hearty eaters).

Hands-on preparation time: 1½ hours
Total preparation time: 2½ hours

☑ Allergy/Intolerance Substitutions:
Tree nuts (coconut): In step 3, replace the 2 Tablespoons (27 g) of coconut cream with 1 Tablespoon (15 ml) of milk of choice. In step 5, replace the coconut water with an equivalent amount of milk of choice.

☑ Reduced Sugar:
There is no added sugar in this recipe.

Filling ingredients:
2 medium-sized russet potatoes (350 g)
1 medium onion (135 g)
1 T. olive oil (15 ml)
2 cloves garlic (12 g)
½ t. kosher salt (3 g)
Black pepper to taste (optional)
2 T. (27 g) coconut cream from one 13.5-oz. (400 ml) can
  of full-fat coconut milk

Dough ingredients:
1 c. gluten free flour mix (130 g)
⅔ c. quinoa flour or bean flour (80 g)
⅓ c. sweet rice flour (44 g)
½ t. table salt (3 g)
¼ c. water (59 ml)
½ c. coconut water (118 ml)
2 T. potato, arrowroot, or tapioca starch (15 g) for dusting

Directions:
Step 1. Peel the potatoes and cut into 1-inch (2.5 cm) cubes. Put the potato cubes in a sauce pan, cover them with water, and place the sauce pan on the stove over **medium-high** heat. After the water comes to a boil, reduce the heat to **medium-low** and simmer for about **20 minutes** till the potatoes are easily pierced with a fork. Drain the potatoes in a colander and then put them back into the dry sauce pan. Mash with a fork or potato masher till nearly smooth (do not use a food processor to mash the potatoes – it will release too much starch and make the filling gummy in texture).

Step 2. Put 1 tablespoon (15 ml) of olive oil in a frying pan; turner the burner to **medium**. Peel and mince the onion; sauté in 1 Tablespoon (15 ml) of olive oil till translucent and lightly browned. Crush the garlic cloves and sauté with the onions for **1 minute** more. Remove from the burner.

Step 3. Add the onion/garlic mixture to the mashed potatoes along with the kosher salt, black pepper (to taste; optional), and 2 tablespoons (27 g) of coconut cream. Continue to mash the potatoes till the mixture is smooth and creamy. Place the potatoes in a glass container, cover, and set aside at room temperature.

Step 4. For the dough, add the gluten free flour mix, quinoa or bean flour, sweet rice flour, and table salt to the bowl of a large food processor. Pulse to combine.

Step 5. Add ¼ cup of water and ½ cup of coconut water to the dry ingredients in the food processor. Process for **1 minute** till the dough comes together into a ball. Let the dough rest at room temperature, covered in the food processor, for **20 minutes**.

Step 6. Sprinkle a large baking pan with 2 Tablespoons (15 g) of potato, arrowroot, or tapioca starch; shake the pan side-to-side to coat the inside of the pan with the starch. Place 2 Tablespoons (30 ml) of water in a small bowl.

Step 7. Lay a large piece of plastic wrap (approximately 12" x 15" or 30 cm x 38 cm in size) on the counter. Place half of the dough on the plastic wrap; lay a second piece of plastic wrap on top of the dough. Keeping the dough between the sheets of plastic wrap, roll it out with a rolling pin till it is ⅛-inch (3 mm) thick. Peel off the top sheet of plastic wrap.

Step 8. Using a 3.5" (9 cm) diameter round cookie cutter or metal jar lid, cut out circles of dough but leave them in place on the bottom layer of plastic wrap. Remove any dough scraps from between the dough circles and set these scraps aside for use in step 10.

Step 9. Place 1 Tablespoon (15 g) of the mashed potato mixture in the center of each circle. Dip a fingertip in the bowl of water and lightly wet the outer edge of one dough circle. Gently fold the dough circle in half over the filling, forming a half-moon shape (if needed, use the bottom piece of plastic wrap to lift one side of the dough circle as you fold). With wet fingertips, pinch the edges of the half-circle together to *completely* seal the dumpling. Gently crimp the edge with a fork (be careful not to pierce the dough with the fork). Place the dumpling in the starch-dusted baking pan.

Step 10. Repeat step 9 for the remaining dough circles. Knead together any left-over dough scraps and roll out to make more pierogi. Cover the pierogi with plastic wrap and refrigerate for **1 hour** to chill.

Step 11. About **30 minutes** before you wish to serve the pierogi, bring 4 quarts (3.8 liters) of water in a large saucepan to a boil. Gently place **half** of the pierogi in the boiling water. Boil them for about **1 minute**, and then flip them over and cook for another **2 minutes**, stirring occasionally to prevent the pierogi from sticking to the bottom of the pot or to each other. (Note: the pierogi will float to the surface of the water and puff up slightly as they cook.) Remove the cooked pierogi from the water and place them on a plate. Repeat this step for the remaining uncooked pierogi.

Step 12. Pierogi can be eaten plain (after boiling), with a sauce, or sautéed with onion. To sauté them with onion, chop one large onion into ¼-inch-square (6-mm-square) pieces. Place the onion in a large non-stick frying pan with 2 Tablespoons (30 ml) of olive oil over **medium** heat. Sauté the onion till it becomes soft, translucent, and begins to brown along the edges. Spread the onion over the bottom of the frying pan. Place half of the boiled pierogis on top of the onion (the onion will prevent the pierogis from sticking to the pan). Sprinkle with kosher salt and powdered garlic. Fry for **1 minute** and then carefully flip the pierogi over and fry for **1 minute** more. Remove the pierogi from the pan, and place on a large serving platter. Repeat this step for the remaining pierogis (be sure to leave about half of the onion in the bottom of the frying pan for the second batch of pierogis). Serve immediately.

☑ Nutritional Content:

Makes 3 servings (about 5 to 6 plain perogies per serving).
Each serving contains: Calories (512 kcal); Total Fat (8 g); Saturated Fat (2 g); Cholesterol (0 g); Sodium (1036 mg); Potassium (682 mg); Total Carbohydrate (99 g); Dietary Fiber (6 g); Sugars (10 g); Protein (10 g) Nutrient(s) of note: Calcium (56 mg), Iron (3.7 mg), Magnesium (35 mg), Phosphorus (89 mg), Potassium (682 mg).

Entrees

Egg-free Cauliflower Pizza

I love cauliflower pizza — it combines America's favorite snack food (pizza) with one very nutritious veggie (cauliflower is loaded with Vitamins C and K, as well as many other nutrients). Unfortunately, most recipes for cauliflower pizza also require eggs as a binder — a problem for those of us who are egg intolerant. This recipe (originally published on my website[5]) uses the gluten free flour mix as the binder. The crust comes out darker than a traditional pizza crust due to the caramelization of the cauliflower. You will need a food processor to make this recipe. Makes enough for one 12" to 16" (40 cm) diameter pizza.

Hands-on preparation time: 30 minutes
Total preparation time: 2 hours 30 minutes

---

[5] Recipe source: Kuehn, D. (2019). www.badcatbakingcompany.com

☑ Allergy/Intolerance Substitutions:
This recipe does not contain any of the eight FDA-identified major allergens or corn.

☑ Reduced Sugar:
There is no added sugar in this recipe.

Ingredients:
1 medium-sized head of cauliflower
1 c. gluten free flour mix (130 g)
1 t. garlic powder (optional; 3 g)
½ t. baking powder (2.5 g)
½ t. table salt (3 g)
2 T. olive oil or other neutral-flavored oil (30 ml)

Directions:
Step 1. Wash the head of cauliflower and pat it dry with a paper towel. Cut the florets off of the cauliflower head, discarding the inner core. You will need 16 to 18 oz. (460 to 530 g) of florets. Cut apart the florets till all are about 1 inch (2.5 cm) in size.

Step 2. Put the florets into a large food processor. Process the cauliflower florets till they are finely ground.

Step 3. Pour the ground cauliflower into a microwave-safe bowl. Microwave for **5 minutes**. Stir the cauliflower with a rubber spatula. Microwave for **3 minutes** more.

Step 4. Line a cookie sheet with parchment paper. Pour the hot cauliflower onto the parchment-lined sheet, and spread it out into a thin layer, breaking up clumps. Let it cool for a minimum of **1 hour** at room temperature.

Step 5. Once cool, pour the cauliflower into a large mixing bowl (discard the wet parchment paper). Add the gluten free flour mix, garlic powder, baking powder, and table salt to the ground cauliflower; mix well with a rubber spatula till the flour is no longer visible. Add the oil and stir to combine.

Step 6. **Pre-heat the oven to 400° F/204° C**. Spray a pizza pan with cooking spray.

Step 7. Knead the dough with your hands for **1 minute**, and then place it on the pizza pan. Using your fingertips, flatten the dough into a pizza shape that is 12 to 16 inches (40 cm) in diameter and ¼" (6 mm) thick. Be sure to make the edge of the pizza a little thicker to form a nice crust.

Step 8. Place the pan in the oven and bake for **40 minutes** till the crust is a dark golden brown and crisp (note: to prevent a soggy crust, do *not* shorten the baking time).

Step 9. Remove the pan from the oven and top as you like with sauce, vegan cheese, and veggies. (Note: if you don't tolerate tomato sauce, use either the Fresh Basil-Parsley Pesto on page 123 or the Roasted Red Pepper Sauce on page 119). Put the pizza pan back in the oven and bake for **15 minutes** more to cook the toppings. Remove from the oven, cool **5 minutes**, and serve.

☑ Nutritional Content:
Makes 8 servings (1 slice per serving, toppings excluded).
Each serving contains: Calories (101 kcal); Total Fat (4 g); Saturated Fat (0.5 g); Cholesterol (0 mg); Sodium (248 mg); Total Carbohydrate (16 g); Dietary Fiber (2 g); Sugars (1 g); Protein (2 g). Nutrient(s) of note: Vitamin C (29 mg), Calcium (51 mg), Vitamin K (11 mcg), Potassium (198 mg).

Laura's Chicken Piccata

This delicious recipe is courtesy of my sister, Laura Cinquemani-Rojahn. Perfect for any night of the week or special occasions, this recipe is quick to prepare and loaded with flavor from the lemon juice and garlic. For those who tolerate dairy, the original recipe uses butter in place of the shortening. Makes 4 light servings.

Hands-on preparation time: 40 minutes
Total preparation time: 40 minutes

☑ **Allergy/Intolerance Substitutions:**
<u>Corn:</u> In step 8, use tapioca starch in place of the corn starch.

☑ **Reduced Sugar:**
There is no added sugar in this recipe.

Chicken filet ingredients:
2 chicken breast halves, skin removed
1 t. kosher salt (6 g)
½ t. ground black pepper (optional; 1 g)
2 T. extra virgin olive oil (30 ml)
1 T. shortening or lard (9 g)
⅓ c. gluten free flour mix (47 g)

Sauce ingredients:
1 T. extra virgin olive oil (15 ml)
1 large garlic clove, crushed (10 g)
½ c. GF SF chicken broth (118 ml)
¼ c. freshly-squeezed lemon juice (59 ml) from 3 lemons
1 t. corn starch or tapioca starch (3 g)
1 whole lemon
1 T. fresh chopped parsley (2 g)

Directions:
Step 1. Place both breast halves flat on a poultry cutting board. Starting at the thickest end of the breast, slice through the chicken breast halves horizontally to make four thin chicken filets.

Step 2. Sprinkle the kosher salt and pepper on both sides of each chicken filet.

Step 3. Put 2 Tablespoons (30 ml) of extra virgin olive oil and the shortening into a large frying pan. Turn the burner to **medium** to melt the shortening and heat the pan.

Step 4. Place the gluten free flour mix in a shallow dish or pie plate. Test the oil to see if the pan is hot enough by sprinkling a pinch of the flour in the pan; when the flour begins to sizzle, proceed to the next step.

Step 5. Dredge the chicken in the gluten free flour mix, coating both sides of each filet; gently shake them to remove any excess flour. Place the filets in the heated oil, and fry till the bottom of each filet has browned. Using tongs, flip each filet over and brown the other side (reduce the heat if the filets begin to brown too quickly). When the thickest part of each filet has reached an internal temperature of **165° F/74° C**, remove it from the pan and place on a plate.

Step 6. Clean and dry the frying pan, and then place it back on the stove over **medium-low heat**. Add 1 Tablespoon (15 ml) of extra virgin olive oil and the crushed garlic. After the garlic begins to sizzle, sauté it for **30 seconds**, stirring constantly with a rubber spatula to prevent it from sticking to the pan.

Step 7. Add the chicken broth to the pan and stir with a rubber spatula to mix the garlic into the broth.

Step 8. Pour the lemon juice into a small bowl; add the corn starch or tapioca starch and whisk to completely dissolve the starch. Add the lemon juice and starch to the frying pan with the broth. Continue to whisk the juice/broth mixture as you bring it to a gentle simmer. Simmer for **3 to 4 minutes**; the sauce will begin to thicken.

Step 9. Using tongs, place the chicken filets back into the frying pan with the sauce. Gently heat one side of the filets in the sauce for **2 minutes** over **medium-low heat** (do not flip the filets over). The sauce will continue to thicken as the filets are heated.

Step 10. Remove the filets from the frying pan with tongs, and place them on a serving platter. Cut the whole lemon into thin slices. Place one or two slices of lemon on each filet, then spoon a little of the sauce from the pan on top. Sprinkle with the chopped parsley. Enjoy!

☑ Nutritional Content:
Makes 4 servings (1 thin chicken filet per serving).
Each serving contains: Calories (263 kcal); Total Fat (15 g); Saturated Fat (3 g); Cholesterol (61 mg); Sodium (822 mg); Total Carbohydrate (12 g); Dietary Fiber (1 g); Sugars (0.5 g); Protein (20 g). Nutrient(s) of note: Vitamin A (69 IU), Magnesium (27 mg), Potassium (318 mg), Phosphorus (187 mg).

Empanadas

Empanadas are small, half-moon-shaped pies that make a delicious side dish or main course. They can be made with either a sweet or savory filling (two different fillings are provided at the end of this recipe, or you can create your own filling). Though often deep fried, these empanadas are baked. Makes 12 small empanadas.

Hands-on preparation time: 40 minutes
Total preparation time: 2 hours and 20 minutes (includes preparing and chilling the filling)

☑ Allergy/Intolerance Substitutions:
<u>Corn:</u> Replace the corn flour with quinoa flour in step 2.
<u>Egg:</u> Leave off the egg wash in step 10, or use the egg wash substitute on page 22.
<u>Porcine/Bovine:</u> In step 2, use agar powder instead of powdered gelatin.

☑ Reduced Sugar:
In step 4, leave out the maple syrup or honey for an unsweetened dough, or replace with 20 drops of alcohol-free liquid stevia if a sweet dough is desired.

Dough ingredients
1 c. gluten free flour mix (130 g)
½ c. corn flour (<u>not</u> corn meal; 62 g)
½ c. arrowroot starch or tapioca starch (60 g)
2 T. quinoa flour or bean flour (15 g)
1½ t. baking powder (7.5 g)
1 t. unflavored, powdered gelatin or agar (2.5 g)
½ t. table salt (3 g)
1½ t. garlic powder (4.5 g)
½ t. dried parsley (0.5 g)
3 T. shortening (27 g)
½ c. water (118 ml)
2 T. olive oil or other neutral-flavored oil (30 ml)
2 T. maple syrup (30 ml) or honey (44 g)
2 T. apple cider vinegar or white distilled vinegar (30 ml)
1 egg for egg wash (optional)

Directions:
Step 1. Prepare one of the fillings on pages 101 and 102, cover, and place in the refrigerator till it is used in step 7.

Step 2. Mix together all of the dry ingredients (including the garlic powder and dried parsley) in a large mixing bowl or the bowl of a large food processor.

Step 3. Cut the shortening into the dry ingredients with a pastry cutter or by pulsing in the food processor until the shortening is completely integrated with the flour mixture.

Step 4. In a medium-sized mixing bowl, whisk together the water, 2 Tablespoons (30 ml) of oil, maple syrup or honey, and vinegar. Pour this liquid into the bowl with the dry ingredients; mix well with your hands or the food processor to form a thick dough. Form the dough into a ball shape and wrap it in a piece of wax paper; let it rest at room temperature for **20 minutes**.

Step 5. Line two cookie sheets with parchment paper. Take the bowl of filling out of the refrigerator and remove its cover. Fill a small bowl with some water.

Step 6. Place a 12" x 12" (30 cm x 30 cm) sheet of plastic wrap on the counter. Place the dough on the plastic wrap, and another sheet of plastic wrap on top of the dough. Roll out the dough till it is ¼-inch (6-mm) thick. Peel off and set aside the top sheet of plastic wrap. Using a 3.5-inch (9 cm) round jar lid or English muffin ring, cut out circles of dough.

Step 7. Place one dough circle on the parchment-lined cookie sheet. Using a small cookie dough scooper, place 1 Tablespoon (16 g) of filling in the center of the circle of dough. Dip a fingertip in the small bowl of water and wet the edge of half of the circle of dough. Gently fold the other half of the circle over the filling, lining up the edges, to form a semi-circle. Gently pinch the edges of the dough together to seal the empanada; crimp the edge gently with a fork (be careful not to pierce the empanada). Repeat this step for the remaining dough circles.

Step 8. Knead together any remaining scraps of dough, roll out the dough between the sheets of plastic wrap, cut more dough circles, and fill them as directed in step 7. Repeat until all of the dough has been used.

Step 9. **Pre-heat the oven to 375° F/190° C.** Use a fork to poke the top of each empanada once (this will allow steam to release during the baking process).

Step 10. Whisk together one egg and 1 Tablespoon (15 ml) of water to make an egg wash, or use the Egg Wash Substitute recipe on page 22. Brush the top of each empanada with the egg wash.

Step 11. Place the cookie sheets in the oven. Bake **25 to 27 minutes** till the empanadas turn golden brown. Remove from the oven and cool for **10 minutes**. Serve with the condiments of your choice.

☑ Nutritional Content:

Empanadas with Sweet Potato Filling: Makes 12 servings (1 empanada containing 1 Tablespoon or 16 g of filling per serving).
Each serving contains: Calories (163 kcal); Total Fat (6 g); Saturated Fat (1 g); Cholesterol (15 mg); Sodium (271 mg); Total Carbohydrate (25 g); Dietary Fiber (2 g); Sugars (4 g); Protein (2 g). Nutrient(s) of note: Vitamin A (126 IU), Calcium (135 mg), Magnesium (46 mg), Potassium (61 mg).

Empanadas with Black Bean Salsa Filling: Makes 12 servings (1 empanada containing 1 Tablespoon or 16 g of filling per serving).
Each serving contains: Calories (183 kcal); Total Fat (7 g); Saturated Fat (1 g); Cholesterol (0 mg); Sodium (407 mg); Total Carbohydrate (26 g); Dietary Fiber (3 g); Sugars (3 g); Protein (3 g). Nutrient(s) of note: Vitamin A (26 IU), Beta-carotene (53 mcg), Calcium (146 mg), Iron (1 mg), Potassium (61 mg).

Sweet Potato Filling for Empanadas

This sweet filling has just a hint of heat. For those with a Nightshade family sensitivity, leave out the red bell pepper and hot pepper sauce.

Ingredients:
1 medium sweet potato (190 to 200 g)
1 small onion (100 g)
¼ c. chopped red bell pepper (30 g)
1 T. olive oil (15 ml)
2 cloves garlic, crushed (15 g)
¼ t. hot pepper sauce (1 ml)
½ t. kosher salt (3 g)
2 T. chopped, fresh cilantro (2 g)

Directions:
Step 1. Peel the sweet potato and cut into half-inch-wide (1-cm-wide) slices. Place the slices in a pot and cover with water. Bring the water to a boil over **medium heat**; boil the potatoes until tender (about **20 minutes**). Drain the sweet potatoes, return to the pot, and cool to release any steam. Mash the potatoes with a fork or potato masher.

Step 2. Add the olive oil to a frying pan. Chop the onion into ¼-inch (6-mm) pieces; add it and the chopped bell pepper to the frying pan and sauté till lightly browned. Add the crushed garlic and sauté **30 seconds** more. Remove from the heat.

Step 3. Add the mashed sweet potatoes, hot pepper sauce, kosher salt, and chopped cilantro to the sauteed onions and peppers; mix well. Place the mixture in a bowl, cover, and chill in the refrigerator for **30 minutes**. Fill the empanadas as directed in the empanada recipe.

Black Bean Salsa Filling for Empanadas

This savory, vegan filling has a little heat from the chipotle pepper powder. For those with a nightshade family sensitivity, leave out the chipotle chile pepper powder and salsa (add 1 Tablespoon of water if leaving out the salsa).

Ingredients:
1 small onion (about 2.5 oz. or 70 g)
2 T. olive oil (30 ml)
1 can of unseasoned black beans, rinsed and drained (15.5 oz. or 439 g)
¼ c. salsa of choice (62 g)
1 t. garlic powder (3 g)
½ t. ground cumin (1.5 g)
½ t. kosher salt (3 g)
¼ t. chipotle chile pepper powder (0.5 g)

Directions:
Step 1. Chop the onion into ¼-inch (6-mm) pieces. Pour the olive oil into a frying pan. Sauté the onions in the oil over **medium heat** till they soften and become translucent (about **2 minutes**).

Step 2. Blot dry the black beans; add them to the onions in the frying pan. Add the salsa and spices to the beans and onions, and stir with a rubber spatula for **2 minutes** to heat through. Using the back of a fork, mash the beans.

Step 3. Pour the bean mixture into a bowl, cover the bowl, and chill in the refrigerator for **30 minutes**. Fill the empanadas as directed in the empanada recipe.

Crispy Fried Chicken

Delicious fried chicken is easy to make with the gluten-free flour mix. The crust on this chicken comes out light and crispy. For a thicker crust, dredge the chicken in a light coating of tapioca starch or potato starch before dipping in the coconut milk in step 5. For chicken tenders (see photo below), use skinless chicken breasts that have been sliced into 1-inch (2.5 cm) strips. This recipe makes enough coating for an entire chicken (cut into parts).

Hands-on preparation time: 60 minutes
Total preparation time: 60 minutes

☑ **Allergy/Intolerance Substitutions:**
<u>Nightshade family:</u> Leave out the paprika in step 2.
<u>Tree nuts (coconut):</u> Replace the coconut milk in steps 3 and 4 with any thick milk that you tolerate.

☑ Reduced Sugar:
Use coconut sugar instead of brown sugar (coconut sugar has a lower glycemic index), or leave out completely.

Ingredients:
2 quarts neutral-flavored oil (1.9 liters) with a high smoke point
1 c. gluten free flour mix (130 g)
¼ c. quinoa flour or brown rice flour (30 g)
2 t. table salt (12 g)
1 T. garlic powder (9 g)
1 t. paprika (3 g)
1 t. onion powder (3 g)
½ t. ground thyme (1.5 g)
½ t. ground black pepper (1.5 g; optional)
½ t. coconut sugar or brown sugar (1.5 g)
1 c. coconut milk (full fat; 237 ml)
1 skin-on chicken, cut into parts

Directions:
Step 1. Pour the oil into a large saucepan or frying pan, and heat over a **medium** burner (the oil should reach **350° F/177° C** by step 5).

Step 2. As the oil is heating, mix together the flours, spices, and sugar in a pie plate.

Step 3. Pour the coconut milk into a separate medium-sized, microwave-safe bowl. Make sure the cream in the coconut milk has not separated from the coconut water. If separation has occurred, warm the coconut milk in a microwave for **1 minute** and then stir to combine.

Step 4. Remove 2 Tablespoons (30 ml) of coconut milk from the bowl and drizzle it over the flour/spice mix. Use your fingers to mix it into the dry ingredients (note: do not overmix; leave in small lumps of flour to give a bumpy texture to the finished chicken).

Step 5. Once the oil has reached **350° F/177° C**, dip a piece of chicken in the coconut milk and then lay it in the flour mix. Cover the top of the chicken with some flour and lightly pat the flour in place on the chicken. Use a fork to gently lift the piece of chicken and place it in the heated oil. Repeat this step for four other pieces of chicken, leaving some space between the pieces of chicken in the frying pan to ensure even frying.

Step 6. After the bottom of the chicken is brown and crisp (about **10 minutes**), turn the pieces over to cook the other side for approximately another **10 minutes** (large pieces such as breast halves with the bone in might require longer frying times). Once the internal temperature of each piece has reached **165° F/74° C**, use metal tongs to remove the pieces of chicken from the oil; place them on a paper towel-lined plate to drain.

Step 7. Repeat steps 5 and 6 for any remaining pieces of chicken. Be sure to bring the oil temperature back to **350° F/177° C** before frying the additional pieces of chicken. Cool for **5 to 6 minutes** before serving.

☑ Nutritional Content:

Makes 8 servings (1 piece of chicken per serving).
Each serving contains: Calories (538 kcal); Total Fat (43 g); Saturated Fat (13 g); Cholesterol (65 mg); Sodium (742 mg); Total Carbohydrate (18 g); Dietary Fiber (1 g); Sugars (0 g); Protein (21 g). Nutrient(s) of note: Vitamin A (192 IU), Phosphorus (41 mg), Potassium (105 mg).

Not-Your-Childhood Fish Cakes

These are not the frozen fish cakes that many of us grew up with! Instead, think of tender chunks of flakey fish mixed with crisp veggies and mild sweet potato, all wrapped in a crispy coating of panko – egg-free too! I use a store-bought GF DF SF panko (e.g., 4C® plain GF panko) for this recipe. Bread crumbs can be used in place of the panko, but do not provide the same crunch as the panko. The fish can be replaced with peeled chunks of shrimp if desired. Makes 8 patties, enough for 4 light eaters.

Hands-on preparation time: 45 minutes
Total preparation time: 45 minutes

☑ **Allergy/Intolerance Substitutions:**
<u>Tree nuts (coconut):</u> In step 5, use a milk of choice other than coconut milk.
<u>Fish:</u> Avoid this recipe.

☑ Reduced Sugar:
There is no added sugar in this recipe.

Ingredients:
1 small sweet potato (about 5 oz.; 142 g)
2 filets of haddock, salmon, cod, or other flakey fish
    (approximately 12 oz. or 340 g total)
2 celery ribs, minced (80 g)
1 scallion, minced (9 g)
1 shallot, minced (12 g)
2 T. chopped fresh parsley (4 g)
3 T. gluten free flour mix (24 g)
½ t. plus ½ t. kosher salt (3 g plus 3 g)
¼ c. pure olive oil (NOT extra virgin) or other neutral-
    flavored oil with a high smoke point (59 ml)
¾ c. GF-DF-SF panko (42 g)
2 t. dry parsley flakes (2 g)
¼ c. full-fat coconut milk or other thick milk of choice (59
    ml)

Directions:
Step 1. Peel and dice the sweet potato into ¼-inch-square (6-mm-square) cubes. Spread the cubes out in a small microwave-safe bowl; microwave for **2 minutes**. Remove the bowl from the microwave and let it cool at room temperature for **2 minutes**.

Step 2. Remove the skin and bones (if present) from the fish filets. Slice the fish into cubes that are about ½-inch-square (1-cm-square) in size. Place them in a large mixing bowl.

Step 3. Add the cooled sweet potato, minced celery, minced scallion, minced shallot, chopped parsley, gluten free flour, and ½ teaspoon (3 g) of kosher salt to the mixing bowl with the fish. Mix well with a rubber spatula till all of the ingredients are well combined. Let the mixture rest at room temperature for **3 minutes**.

Step 4. As the fish and vegetable mixture rests, pour the oil into a large frying pan. Heat the oil over a **medium heat** till a crumb placed in the oil begins to sizzle.

Step 5. As the oil heats, mix together the panko, dry parsley flakes, and ½ teaspoon (3 g) of kosher salt in a large bowl or pie pan. Pour the coconut milk into a separate small bowl.

Step 6. Using a large cookie scooper, scoop out about 2 Tablespoons (42 g) of the fish mixture and release it into one of your hands. Press the mixture together between your hands to create a patty-shape.

Step 7. Wet the fingertips of one hand with the coconut milk and dab it onto both sides of the fish patty. (Note: these patties are delicate so dipping them into the coconut milk could make them fall apart). Gently place the patty in the dish of panko. Sprinkle panko on top of the fish patty and pat it into place; make sure the bottom and sides are well-coated with the panko also. Place the patty into the heated oil. Repeat steps 6 and 7 for the remaining fish mixture.

Step 8. Let the patties cook over **medium heat** till the bottoms are crisp and brown. Using a metal spatula, gently flip each patty over to brown the other side.

Step 9. Line a large plate with a paper towel. Once the bottom of each patty is golden brown, check to make sure each is firm to the touch and has reached an internal temperature of **145° F/63° C**. Gently remove each patty from the oil and place on the paper-towel-lined plate. Enjoy these fish patties warm.

☑ Nutritional Content:

Makes 4 servings (2 fish cakes per serving).

Each serving contains: Calories (319 kcal); Total Fat (17 g); Saturated Fat (5 g); Cholesterol (47 mg); Sodium (727 mg); Total Carbohydrate (22 g); Dietary Fiber (2 g); Sugars (2 g); Protein (19 g). Nutrient(s) of note: Vitamin A (5,386 IU), Beta-carotene (3,319 mcg), Calcium (41 mg), Iron (1.7 mg), Phosphorus (210 mg), Potassium (646 mg).

Sauces and Extras

Turkey Meatballs

Yes, you can make meatballs without the eggs! The trick is to add a little flour to work as a binder. The addition of finely chopped mushrooms keeps these meatballs moist and flavorful. Makes 12 meatballs.

Hands-on preparation time: 15 minutes
Total preparation time: 1 hour and 15 minutes (includes the 30 minutes needed to soak the dried shitake mushrooms)

☑ **Allergy/Intolerance Substitutions:**
Does not include any of the eight FDA-identified major allergens or corn.

☑ **Reduced Sugar:**
There is no added sugar in this recipe.

Meatball ingredients:
4 large dried shitake mushrooms (0.5 oz. or 14 g)
1 lb. fresh ground turkey (454 g)
2 T. gluten free flour mix (16 g)
1 T. garlic powder (9 g)
1 T. dried basil (3 g)
1 T. dried parsley (3 g)
1 t. dried oregano (1 g)
1 t. onion powder (3 g)
½ t. black pepper (1.5 g; optional)
½ t. fine sea salt (3 g)
3 T. milk of choice (45 ml)

Pre-heat oven: 350° F/ 177° C

Directions:
Step 1. Rinse and then soak the dried shitakes in 1 cup (237 ml) of warm water for **30 minutes**. Blot dry the shitakes, remove and discard any remaining pieces of stem, and then mince.

Step 2. Add all of the meatball ingredients (including the minced shitake) to a large mixing bowl. Combine by hand till all of the ingredients are well integrated with the ground turkey. Wash your hands.

Step 3. Line a cookie sheet with parchment paper. Using a large cookie scooper, scoop out enough of the meatball mix to completely fill the scooper (about 2 Tablespoons or 32 g). Release the meatball from the scooper, and place it on the parchment-lined cookie sheet. Repeat this step for the remaining meatball mix.

Step 4. Pick up each meatball and roll gently between your hands to form a ball. Place each meatball back onto the parchment, spacing the meatballs about 0.5 inches (1 cm) apart.

Step 5. Place the meatballs in the pre-heated oven and bake for **18 to 22 minutes**, till a thermometer inserted in the largest meatball reads **165° F/74°C** (don't over-bake). Remove the cookie sheet from the oven and cover the meatballs with a sheet of aluminum foil to keep them warm till serving.

☑ Nutritional Content:

Makes 6 servings (2 meatballs per serving; excludes pasta and sauce). Each serving contains: Calories (106 kcal); Total Fat (1 g); Saturated Fat (0 g); Cholesterol (37 mg); Sodium (251 mg); Total Carbohydrate (7 g); Dietary Fiber (1 g); Sugars (0 g); Protein (18 g). Nutrient(s) of note: Iron (1 mg), Potassium (80 mg).

Garlic and Herb Olive Oil Dip

This herbed oil dip is the perfect replacement for butter on bread. Simple and quick to prepare, this dip adds a garlicy touch to the Wholegrain Italian Bread (see page 33). The dried herbs can be replaced with 1 teaspoon of finely chopped fresh basil and parsley. Makes enough for two people.

Hands-on preparation time: 5 minutes
Total Preparation time: 6 minutes

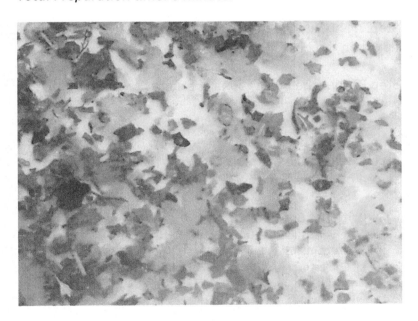

☑ Allergy/Intolerance Substitutions:
This recipe does not include any of the eight FDA-identified allergens or corn.

☑ Reduced Sugar:
There is no added sugar in this recipe.

Ingredients:

1 large garlic clove, peeled (10 g)
½ t. dry basil flakes (0.25 g)
½ t. dry parsley flakes (0.25 g)
½ t. kosher salt (3 g)
¼ t. red pepper flakes (0.25 g)
¼ c. extra virgin olive oil or other oil of choice (59 ml)

Directions:

Step 1. Mash the garlic with a garlic masher, and place it on a small microwave-safe shallow dish or dessert plate.

Step 2. Sprinkle the herbs, kosher salt, and red pepper flakes on the plate with the garlic.

Step 3. Pour the oil on top of the spices and herbs. Stir with a fork to combine.

Step 4. Place the plate in a microwave; heat for **30 seconds**. Remove the plate from the microwave. Serve the spiced oil with warm slices of bread.

☑ Nutritional Content:

Makes 2 servings (about 2 Tablespoons per serving).
Each serving contains: Calories (248 kcal); Total Fat (28 g); Saturated Fat (4 g); Cholesterol (0 g); Total Carbohydrate (2 g); Dietary Fiber (0 g); Sugars (0 g); Sodium (601 mg); Protein (0 g). Nutrient of note: Potassium (29 mg).

Roasted Red Pepper Pasta Sauce

I use this simple sauce as a replacement for tomato-based sauces on pasta and pizza. Easy to prepare, it clings great to pasta and is savory like tomato sauce. The fresh herbs can be replaced with dried herbs. Vegan sausage can be substituted for the meat-based sausage, or leave out the sausage entirely. This recipe works well with the Homemade Italian Sausage on page 127. Makes 3 cups.

Hands-on preparation time: 50 minutes
Total Preparation time: 2 hours and 20 minutes

☑ **Allergy/Intolerance Substitutions:**
<u>Nightshade family</u>: Contains bell peppers; avoid this recipe if needed.

☑ **Reduced Sugar:**
There is no added sugar in this recipe.

Ingredients:
6 large red and/or orange bell peppers (about 1200 g)
2 T. extra virgin olive oil or other oil of choice (30 ml)
⅔ c. chopped onion (75 g)
⅓ c. finely chopped celery (38 g)
2 T. fresh chopped basil (4 g)
1 T. fresh chopped parsley (2 g)
1 c. loose Italian sausage or vegan sausage (about 235 g; optional)

Pre-heat oven: Broil

Directions:
Step 1. Place the whole peppers in a single layer in a large baking pan. Place the pan in the oven, about 6 inches below the broiler. Using metal tongs, turn the peppers **every 4 minutes** until the skin on the peppers is charred and loose (**about 30 to 35 minutes total**). Remove the baking pan from the oven and cool the peppers at room temperature for about **30 minutes**. Alternately, you can roast the peppers on an outdoor grill.

Step 2. Once the peppers have cooled, slice them open lengthwise and remove the stem, core, and seeds (discard these). Peel the loose skin off of each pepper and discard the skin as well.

Step 3. Place the roasted peppers in a blender; **puree for 1 minute** until smooth.

Step 4. In a medium-sized pot, heat the olive oil over **medium heat** for **1 minute**. Add the chopped onion and celery, and sauté till lightly caramelized (about **10 minutes**).

Step 5. Turn the burner down to **medium-low**. Add the pureed pepper, 1 Tablespoon (2 g) of fresh basil, and 1 Tablespoon (2 g) of fresh parsley to the pot with the onions; stir to combine. Cover the pot. Bring the sauce to a simmer, reduce the heat to **low**, and simmer for **1 hour,** stirring every **5 to 10 minutes** to prevent the sauce from burning on the bottom of the pot.

Step 6. As the sauce cooks, sauté the loose Italian sausage in a frying pan till it is cooked through. Drain on a plate lined with paper towel.

Step 7. After the sauce has cooked for **1 hour**, add the cooked sausage and remaining Tablespoon (2 g) of fresh basil; stir and serve immediately over pasta. This sauce freezes and reheats well.

☑ Nutritional Content:

Sauce with meat: Makes 5 servings (about ½ cup per serving, includes turkey sausage, excludes pasta).
Each serving contains: Calories (206 kcal); Total Fat (9 g); Saturated Fat (9 g); Cholesterol (13 mg); Total Carbohydrate (21 g); Dietary Fiber (9 g); Sugars (6 g); Sodium (248 mg); Protein (14 g). Nutrient(s) of note: Vitamin A (926 IU), Beta-Carotene (507 mcg), Calcium (42 mg), Vitamin C (200 mg), Magnesium (62 mg), Phosphorus (213 mg), Potassium (1157 mg).

Sauce without meat: Makes 5 servings (about ½ cup per serving, excludes sausage and pasta).
Each serving contains: Calories (119 kcal); Total Fat (7 g); Saturated Fat (1 g); Cholesterol (0 mg); Total Carbohydrate (14 g); Dietary Fiber (9 g); Sugars (6 g); Sodium (38 mg); Protein (4 g). Nutrient(s) of note: Vitamin A (926 IU), Beta-Carotene (507 mcg), Calcium (42 mg), Vitamin C (200 mg), Magnesium (42 mg), Phosphorus (79 mg), Potassium (658 mg).

Fresh Basil-Parsley Pesto Sauce

Fresh garlic and a touch of red pepper flakes give this pesto a little zing. I like to serve this sauce with Turkey Meatballs (page 113) and Vegan Linguine (page 55), but it can also be used on pizza. Though ground pine nuts are traditionally included in pesto, raw cashews, pumpkin seeds, or sunflower seeds work equally well in this sauce. Makes enough sauce for 4 people.

Hands-on preparation time: 10 minutes
Total preparation time: 20 minutes

☑ Allergy/Intolerance Substitutions:
Tree nuts (pine nuts or cashews): In step 1, leave out the pine nuts or cashews (no replacement is needed), or replace with 1.2 ounces (35 g) raw shelled pumpkin seeds or sunflower seeds.
Nightshade family: Leave out the red pepper flakes in step 2; no replacement is needed.

☑ Reduced Sugar:
There is no added sugar in this recipe.

Pesto ingredients:
¼ c. raw pine nuts, raw cashews, raw sunflower seeds (shells removed), or raw pumpkin seeds (shells removed; 38 g)
1 large garlic clove, peeled (10 g)
1.3 oz. fresh basil leaves (no stems; 37 g)
0.2 oz. fresh parsley (5 g)
5 T. extra virgin olive oil (75 ml)
¼ t. red pepper flakes (0.7 g; optional)
¾ t. kosher salt (4.5 g)

Directions:
Step 1. Place the nuts or seeds in a small baking pan and bake till light brown (about **8 minutes** for pine nuts or seeds, and **10 minutes** for raw cashews) at **350° F/177° C**. Remove the nuts or seeds from the oven; cool for **5 minutes**.

Step 2. Cut the garlic clove in half. Add the garlic and remaining ingredients to the bowl of a large food processor. Pulse the ingredients 5 or 6 times to combine.

Step 3. Scrape the sides of the food processor bowl with a rubber spatula. Food process for **1 minute** more to puree the pesto into a grainy paste.

Step 4. If serving with pasta, heat 2 Tablespoons (30 ml) of extra virgin olive oil for **1 minute over medium heat** in a large frying pan. Reduce the heat to **low**. Add the cooked pasta and sauté with a rubber spatula to coat the pasta with the oil.

Step 5. Add the pesto to the pasta in the frying pan and mix well with a rubber spatula. Sauté **2 to 4 minutes**, stirring frequently, to completely coat the pasta with the pesto and to lightly cook the pesto (note: remove the pan from the heat immediately if the pesto begins to burn). Remove the frying pan from the heat and serve the pasta immediately.

☑ Nutritional Content:

Makes enough pesto for 4 servings of pasta (about 40 g per serving; excludes olive oil and pasta). Each serving contains: Calories (218 kcal); Total Fat (24 g); Saturated Fat (3 g); Cholesterol (0 mg); Total Carbohydrate (3 g); Dietary Fiber (1 g); Sugars (0 g); Sodium (458 mg); Protein (1.5 g). Nutrient(s) of note: Vitamin A (564 IU), Beta-Carotene (329 mcg), Magnesium (20 mg), Potassium (100 mg).

Homemade Italian Sausage

This simple recipe makes excellent Italian sausage. You can grind your own pork and turkey to make the sausage, or take a shortcut like I do and buy it pre-ground. Any unused sausage can be placed in the freezer for future use. For a histamine intolerance diet, leave out the black pepper and crushed red pepper. Makes about 2 pounds (907 g) of sausage.

Hands-on preparation time: 15 minutes
Total preparation time: 15 minutes (does not include cooking time which will vary)

☑ Allergy/Intolerance Substitutions:
<u>Nightshade family:</u> In step 1, leave out the crushed red pepper; no substitution needed.

☑ Reduced Sugar:
There is no added sugar in this recipe.

Sausage ingredients:
1 lb. fresh ground turkey (454 g)
1 lb. fresh ground pork (454 g)
1½ T. dried parsley (5 g)
2 t. dried marjoram or oregano (2 g)
2 t. onion powder (6 g)
2 t. fennel seeds (6 g)
2 t. dried sage (2 g)
1 t. ground thyme (2 g)
1 t. fine sea salt (6 g)
½ t. ground black pepper (1.5 g; optional)
¼ t. crushed red pepper (0.7 g; optional)

Directions:
Step 1. Add all of the sausage ingredients to a large mixing bowl. Combine by hand till all of the herbs and spices are well integrated into the ground turkey and pork. Wash your hands.

Step 2. Use as needed for your recipe. Be sure to heat to **165° F/74°C** before serving.

☑ Nutritional Content:
Makes 6 servings (2 meatballs per serving; excludes pasta and sauce). Each serving contains: Calories (293 kcal); Total Fat (17 g); Saturated Fat (6 g); Cholesterol (91 g); Total Carbohydrate (3 g); Dietary Fiber (1 g); Sugars (0 g); Sodium (472 mg); Protein (31 g). Nutrient(s) of note: Vitamin A (132 IU), Calcium (54 mg), Iron (2 mg), Phosphorus (146 mg), Potassium (281 mg).

About the Author

Diane Kuehn's love of baking took an unplanned turn with a diagnosis of gluten sensitivity in 2008. Unsatisfied with store-bought gluten-free foods, she began experimenting with her own gluten-free flour mix and the creation of gluten-free recipes. As her food intolerances increased to include dairy, soy, eggs, and high-histamine foods, she adapted her recipes to cater to multiple food allergies. Diane is college professor in Central New York State, where she lives with her husband, dog, and cats.

For more information about the author and free recipes to download, visit:
BadCatBakingCompany.com

Made in the USA
Middletown, DE
21 December 2021

54424371R00076